# DELIVER

## GREAT PRODUCTS
## *that*
## CUSTOMERS LOVE

The Guide to Product Management for
Innovators, Leaders, and Entrepreneurs

## Valerio Zanini

5D VISION

5D Vision Publishing

Deliver Great Products That Customers Love

Printed in the United States of America

10 9 8 7 6 5 4 3 2 1

Library of Congress Control Number: 2018906202
ISBN (Hardcover): 978-0-9989854-1-1
ISBN (Paperback): 978-0-9989854-2-8

Hashtag: Follow #DeliverTheBook for updates and comments

We plant one tree for every copy of this book sold, in partnership with ForestPlanet.org

Published in the United States of America by 5D Vision Publishing, an imprint of 5D Vision, LLC. Bulk purchase discounts, special editions, and customized excerpts are available directly from the publisher. For information about a sponsored edition for your company, or books for educational and promotional purposes, please email the publisher at info@5dvision.com

Cover design by: Maxi-1989/99Designs
Cover image: 32 pixels/Shutterstock
Photos and illustrations: © Valerio Zanini, unless noted otherwise

 5D VISION

To my wife Deborah, for all your loving support and for always pushing me to become a better person

To my parents Roberto and Maria, for teaching me the value of hard work and for inspiring me to always try new things

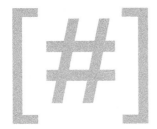

# TABLE OF CONTENTS

# [2] GREAT PRODUCTS COME FROM GREAT PRODUCT MANAGERS    15

# [PART 2] THE THREE PILLARS OF PRODUCT SUCCESS

# [3] KEEP THE CUSTOMER IN FOCUS    27

# [4] INFUSE A CULTURE OF AGILITY    41

# [5] EMPOWER YOUR TEAM 61

# [PART 3] THE FIVE DIMENSIONS

# [6] THE FIVE DIMENSIONS OF PRODUCT MANAGEMENT 71

# [7] DISCOVER  87

# [8] DESIGN  123

# [11] DELIVER                                                217

# APPENDIX                                                    233

# DELIVER

"To produce the promised, desired,
or expected results "

Merriam-Webster dictionary

"Deliver." *Merriam-Webster.com*. Merriam-Webster, n.d. Web. 9 Oct. 2018.

# INTRODUCTION

I love building products. Ever since I was a little kid, I have enjoyed the thrill of solving a problem and building a solution. When I was eleven, with my first computer (a Commodore VIC-20), I developed a software to organize all my personal contacts. At the time, I was already feeling the pain of knowing more than ten people and struggling to organize their information. I dreamed that the software I had written could solve the same problem for other people. As soon as the program was ready, I created a brand, gave it a name, and even decided on a price. I was ready to launch it in the market: my neighborhood.

Just the thought of another person using my tool and finding it useful was exciting. I soon understood that my addressable market was limited as I could not find anyone else with the same computer in my circle of friends. So I kept dreaming of the next opportunity, and the program lived on just for my personal use.

Over the years, I have launched digital products in a variety of organizations, and I still feel the same butterflies and excitement on the eve of every new product's launch. As product managers, we spend months ideating on a new concept, building prototypes, developing the product, and finally getting ready for deployment. It's exhausting yet exciting. All the months of hard work finally converge into an actual "thing" — something tangible we are about to bring to life for the world to enjoy.

And yet this final delivery is only the beginning. The launch of a new product in the market may be the finish line of months of hard work, but it's the starting point of something else. As soon as your product is ready, you begin having real customers, getting their feedback, and learning of a thousand better ways to improve it or to make a new version of it. Suddenly, you enter a new circle of ideation, prototyping, and development. It's like riding on the Ferris wheel at an amusement park or, more often than not, on a roller coaster. As soon as you reach the end, you are set to start it all over again. This is the life of a product manager!

I have met many people who were new to product management or who were interested in making the transition to a new role, and who have asked me for advice. They wanted to learn what it is like to be a product manager and what tools they should use to be more effective. I had the opportunity, and the pleasure, to expose numerous people to new methodologies, organize hands-on exercises, and provide coaching on Design Thinking, Empathy Interviews, Product Journey Maps, and more.

When given the opportunity, I invited them to work with me or my team so they could experience what it is like to be a product manager. If they were really eager to learn more, I would suggest a list of great books they could read to gain a deeper knowledge of the job, and learn different methodologies. Unfortunately, the list was long because no single text offered a comprehensive view of the product manager's role. I could read in their eyes how daunting that mountain of reading was and how overwhelmed they felt at not knowing where to start.

I found it difficult to recommend a single title that would help them understand the role of the product manager and give them exposure to a variety of methodologies they could start implementing right away. There are great books on product management, on Agile, on various methodologies, but I didn't find one that could serve as both an intro for novices, and a reference for experts.

I have also met many entrepreneurs and CEOs who were struggling to build the right product. Some were building their products for the first time; others had already had a successful start and were forced to innovate by the pace of technology or changes in the market. Many had focused all their energy on developing their new product and preparing for its launch, and had lost track of who the real customer was.

Often, these young companies didn't have a strong product management culture in their organization and were striving to understand how to solve their challenges. Product development seemed to be either left to one area of the organization — marketing, sales, IT, etc. — or, at the other end of the spectrum, was still tightly controlled by the founders. It was not infused throughout the organization.

This is where this book comes from. It is for dreamers, for makers, and for entrepreneurs of all stripes, and is designed to inspire a culture of product management in your organization, and to help you understand how to build a great product. It explains why creating a customer-centric focus is important, and the shortfalls of companies that focus on deploying products without a proper understanding of who the real customer is. It references key methodologies that can be applied at any stage of product development, from Discovery to Delivery.

Launching a product is hard work, but it's a rewarding and exciting process. This book explains the key elements every team or organization should have to build great products, and useful methodologies that product managers can employ at each stage of the product development life cycle.

While it is not designed to be a detailed encyclopedia of techniques and all possible applications, my intent is to stimulate your passion for product management, give you enough tools to be able to start applying these techniques in your job, and then provide a reference to other materials you can use to learn more. There are great books on almost every topic you may wish to learn, so there is no value in reinventing the wheel. Instead, wherever useful or necessary, I point to other references that cover a specific topic in greater detail. I invite you to explore these additional resources and learn more about your favorite topic or methodology.

This book is for any person who is responsible for creating a new product or improving an existing one: not only product managers, but also entrepreneurs, founders and CEOs at new startups, user experience and interaction designers, consultants, project managers, and marketing managers. If you are a dreamer and a maker, this book is for you.

In **Part 1**, I discuss the role of the product manager and why it's essential to the success of a product.

**Part 2** is dedicated to the Three Pillars of product success: customer focus, culture of agility, and team empowerment.

In **Part 3**, I present the 5D Vision of Product Management, a framework that helps product managers "see" a product through the five dimensions of Discover, Design, Develop, Deploy and Deliver.

# [PART 1]

## A GREAT PRODUCT

Saint Peter's Cathedral in Rome, Italy

# [1]

# HOW GREAT PRODUCTS ARE BUILT

The meeting with the customer did not go well. The prototype was not yet finished, and the customer wasn't able to grasp the qualities of the idea he was presenting. This project was already over budget, and there was no clear line of sight on its completion. By all measures, it was taking too long to put together, and the customer was getting anxious. He knew he was about to lose his job.

It was the end of 1546 A.D. and the project was the construction of Saint Peter's Cathedral in Rome. It had started 40 years prior, and there was no sign of progress. Several architects had come and gone, and the customer, Pope Paul III was facing increasing criticism over spiraling costs and the endless delays. What was intended to be the symbol of all Christianity was not moving any closer to completion, and the Pope had not yet seen a clear plan to finish it.

The most recent architect, Antonio il Giovane (Anthony the Young), had spent the previous seven years building a gigantic, wooden model that would show in full detail the grandiose plan he intended to pursue.[1] He wanted to have a full representation of the finished work to get the Pope's buy-in on every detail before beginning construction. He intended to fix every detail of the final construction and offer a plan to follow. This was standard practice for the times — no wonder cathedrals took 200 years to complete!

In the modern world, this would be called a Waterfall approach. Imagine spending seven years creating a very detailed prototype covering all the specifics of the planned project, from the broad vision to the specific requirements of every little feature. And once you finally complete it, you find out that it does not satisfy your customer's need.

What happened next is an example of agility and empowerment similar to the cultural shift taking hold today in companies around the world.

Tired of the delays, setbacks, and overall lack of progress, Pope Paul III fired the architect and called on Michelangelo for help. The Pope gave him full authority, empowering the new architect to make any decision on the design, prioritization of the work, and delivery of the project.

Michelangelo immediately discarded the wooden model built by his predecessor and threw away the existing plans. To remove some constraints and establish a more solid foundation for the building, he even tore down parts of the Cathedral that his predecessor had built. With the Pope's full authorization, he set off to design a new concept for the largest church in the world.

In just a few days, he built a clay model of his new concept and shared it with the Pope. The model was a basic, rough representation of the whole plan, intended for quick iteration. He received feedback that the design seemed a bit dark, and Michelangelo promptly modified the window designs to allow for more light to penetrate inside. He again showed the new model to the Pope, and this time his customer liked the general idea.

Compared to a single, fully detailed wooden model like the one his predecessor had built, Michelangelo's clay prototypes allowed for rapid iterations of building and receiving customer feedback. Because he did not waste time on every single detail, but rather built clay models for small portions of the cathedral at a time, Michelangelo was able to get the Pope's feedback very quickly and avoid lengthy changes when something didn't go well.

Today, we have only a handful of plans of St. Peter's from that time. It's not that they were destroyed over time, but rather that Michelangelo simply didn't bother making detailed plans. He conceived, planned, and built a small section of the church at a time. Instead of detailed plans, he used prototypes. He built clay and wooden models that were easy to put together and adjust quickly as needed. When he realized that something was not right, he was ready to tear it down and conceive a new idea. He had an overarching vision for the final cathedral, and he was getting there one step at a time.

Michelangelo worked on Saint Peter's for 17 years, until his death. In this time, he made much more progress than all other architects that had preceded him during the prior 40 years. In doing so, he provided us with, perhaps, the first example of how to employ agility from ideation to execution. And he left behind what is still today one of the world's wonders.

Building the largest church in the world in the 16th century must have required a massive effort without the technology and machinery we have today. Yet, Michelangelo employed several techniques that resemble what today we call Agile, Lean, and iterative development. Rather than wasting time on a detailed, immutable, upfront plan, he built in increments, tested his assumptions, and then decided how best to continue. He pivoted when it was necessary.

In this way, Michelangelo was a great inspiration to today's product managers. He blended technical acumen with a strong sense of design and the capacity to empathize with his customers to understand their needs and build a great product.

Today's methodologies are changing the way product managers approach their work. Agile, Lean Startup, Design Thinking and others let us ideate, plan, and execute new products at a speed and with a confidence that was never possible before. Because these methodologies are condensing the learning cycle and are putting product managers closer to their customers, they can help deliver what customers really need and reduce the risk of building the wrong product.

# VALIDATE AS SOON AS POSSIBLE

A developer approached me at a recent Agile conference where I was presenting a topic on building great products with small iterations, and he said, "*I wish I had known this a year ago....*" He had taken on a new project from a company that provided a full document of requirements upfront. They wanted to build a new system and do it all at once.

Since the requirements clearly explained what the customer wanted, he set off and worked at building the system for the following six months. By the time he was done, the company had gone bankrupt and he was never paid. "*If I had known how to build an MVP (Minimum Viable Product), I would have suggested that to my customer, and I would have built only a small piece of the whole system,*" he added.

This approach to a new project is not different from what has been going on in the industry for a long time. Not even 10 or 15 years ago, and sometimes still today, the traditional way of building a product or a new business followed a combination of some of these steps:

- Ideate a solution and design a new product
- Write a detailed Product Requirements Document
- Find a budget or raise initial capital
- Hire a development team and build the whole system
- Launch the finished product in the market
- Evaluate how sales are going
- Pivot if necessary

Each of these steps was a big hurdle, and developing the system, in particular, was a big and expensive challenge. Often, the challenge is amplified when there is not a single stakeholder and requirements come from different stakeholders that can be (partly) opposite. Reaching agreement on those requirements without an MVP can be a lengthy process.

Without a working system to demonstrate, nor any customers, it was hard to raise capital. This approach also put all the risk at the end, waiting for market validation to know if you had built the right product, often after months of development and a large upfront investment.

The Internet, cloud computing, open-source software, widely available code libraries, and APIs have immensely reduced the effort needed to start a new online business. If before you needed to buy your own servers, install expensive software packages, and

REDUCED RISK, INVESTMENT & COST

write custom code for almost every function of your software, today you can do all this in a leaner and faster way. Not only is your upfront capital investment minimized, but so is the time to market. You can build a prototype of your idea in days instead of months, and quickly make it available to potential customers for feedback and validation.

The technology innovations that made all this possible have transformed how companies approach new projects. But the combined impact of Agile, Lean Startup, and Design Thinking has really shifted the mindset on how to bring an idea to life and achieve market validation without a large upfront investment.

These methodologies have turned the approach upside down. Entrepreneurs now have many more opportunities to build an MVP and validate their ideas. The goal is to validate the business concept, learn from your customers if there is market-solution fit, and if necessary pivot as early as possible. All this without a significant upfront investment of time or money.

Ideally, you could share the concept of your system before you build anything, find early adopters, and get their feedback. Would they buy your product or service? Market validation is the most important step in building a product, and the earlier you can achieve it, the better.

**Uber** made a partnership with a local black car rental company in San Francisco and tested the concept of reserving a car ride with an app. It had to build just a simple version of its app as the rides were provided by the partner company. The test was quick and simple, yet it allowed Uber to validate the customer demand for its service before investing in building its own network of drivers.

**Groupon** famously started with a WordPress blog that was edited once a day to describe the new offers available to customers. A FileMaker database running offline on one of the founders' computers kept track of the orders, which were serviced by hand one by one. It was quick to build and helped validate the business concept before committing to a larger investment and building the full web capability.

The goal of every team should be to find the fastest, cheapest, easiest way to test and validate a new idea and get to market-solution fit as quickly as possible. Once you know that you have found a rough diamond, then you can commit to building a team and investing in creating a shiny product.

Ideating, building, and validating your ideas without large upfront investments is a common theme throughout this book, and it's at the core of a culture of agility.

# THE THREE PILLARS OF PRODUCT SUCCESS

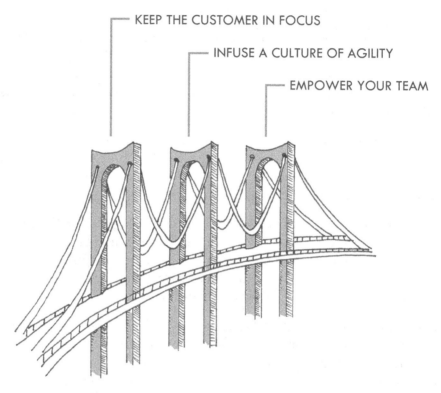

KEEP THE CUSTOMER IN FOCUS

INFUSE A CULTURE OF AGILITY

EMPOWER YOUR TEAM

The product's success is built upon the three pillars of customer focus, agility, and team empowerment

I have worked in a variety of organizations across different industries, helping my teams or my clients build successful products. From Cisco to Capital One, from my startup Goozex.com to clients I have advised, from private organizations to the military, I have found three common elements that successful teams must have to deliver great products. These elements are the three pillars of a strong customer focus, a culture of agility, and an empowered team.

I believe that these three pillars are what sustain every successful team in building great products. Organizations and teams that keep their customer needs in focus, foster a culture of agility, and empower their teams to make the right decisions, are more likely to set the conditions for great products to come alive.

## KEEP THE CUSTOMER IN FOCUS

Maintaining a customer focus defines the product manager's attitude of seeking and incorporating the customer's input into his or her decisions at every step in the product development cycle. This should not be relegated to the Discovery phase, but rather should be an essential activity throughout the development and launch of a product.

Asking for customer feedback at every step allows the manager to identify needs and define the proper solution. Customers buy a solution to their needs in the form of a customer experience, and only by maintaining the focus on their needs you can build the right product.

## INFUSE A CULTURE OF AGILITY

To compete in today's market, companies need to be nimble, fast, and able to adapt to changing conditions. Like the wooden model built by the architect prior to Michelangelo, which had taken over seven years to complete only to discover that the customer was no longer interested in that plan, companies cannot afford to spend a long time planning and building a product that is perfect in every single detail. By the time they are done, the market has likely either found something else, or has changed.

A timeless example of this is when Philips, a large electronics manufacturer based in the Netherlands, introduced a new video cassette recorder in the market. It was the Video 2000 and it came right in the middle of the "videotape format war" already taking place between VHS and Betamax.[2] From a technical point of view, Video 2000 offered superior quality and a few innovative features. However, Philips' competitors JVC and Sony (makers of the VHS and Betamax formats respectively) had been in the market already for at least five years. Despite a less advanced system, VHS had 70% of market share for domestic video recorders worldwide. Nobody wanted to buy the Video 2000 system for which there were no movies available. Philips had simply taken too long to build its system and it was too late.

Companies need to keep the cost of change, and the associated risk, as low as possible, while building the best solution to the customer's needs. Agile allows you to break product development in small iterations and to incorporate customer feedback at each step. But adopting Agile methods is not enough if the underlying culture does not support a culture of agility. By building an ethos of transparency, inspection, and adaptation, companies can use short development cycles and adjust their plans quickly to match the customer needs. Agility needs to span all phases of development, from ideation to launch. Cross-functional teams can build products in small increments, proceeding from idea to launch in a matter of weeks rather than months and learning from their customers quickly. They can adapt based on the learning, and prepare for the next iteration.

Employing agility across the full product development cycle allows companies to develop their 5D Vision, which is a foundation for a culture of agility.

## EMPOWER YOUR TEAM

Empowerment is about trusting your employees to make the right decisions. Leaders need to act as servant leaders toward their teams. By delegating decision-making authority and giving employees the context and resources to make decisions, leaders foster an environment where better solutions are created, and team morale is increased. Empowerment is at all levels in the product organization, from the leaders to the developers, to the customers.

Part 2 of this book is dedicated to the three pillars of product success.

# THE 5D VISION OF A PRODUCT

Sometimes product development goes through several phases each managed by different areas of the organization and in sequential steps. Even if the work within a single area uses Agile (in IT, for example), the overall product development process is still waterfall.

Companies cannot afford to manage projects as a sequential list of phases. Product development should be managed as a cross-dimensional project to break the silos between each phase and reduce the risk of dependencies.

Product managers should not work on one dimension at a time, move on to the next one when ready, and hope that everything flows nicely. They should employ a 5-Dimensional vision of their product. This requires looking at a product from the 5 dimensions of:

**Discover, Design, Develop, Deploy, Deliver**

This book describes a framework called the 5D Vision of Product Management. It helps product managers broaden their practice beyond the traditional Software Development Life Cycle, and look at a product as a set of attributes that deliver a great customer experience. By focusing on each of the five dimensions of the 5D Vision, product managers can plan and execute great products that customers love.

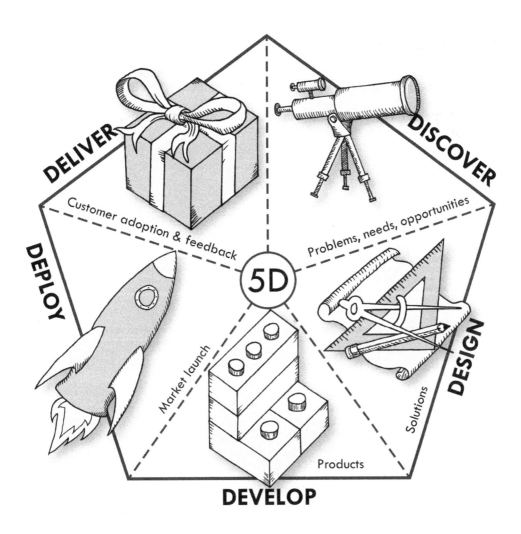

The 5 Dimensions of Product Management: Discover,
Design, Develop, Deploy, Deliver

Part 3 of this book is dedicated to the 5D Vision of Product Management.

# REFERENCES

1.  Mauro Mussolin et al., *Michelangelo architetto a Roma*, Silvana Editoriale, 2010

2.  "Videotape format war", Wikipedia https://www.wikipedia.org/wiki/Videotape_format_war

# NOTES

A Ferrari sunbathing in the streets of Naples, Italy

# [2]

# GREAT PRODUCTS COME FROM GREAT PRODUCT MANAGERS

What makes a product great? Is it its features? Its quality? Its beauty? Or maybe its price? Certainly, these characteristics are valuable and contribute to making a successful product. One could argue that products should have all of them to be successful. After all, who wants to buy something that doesn't work, or that's ugly? Some products focus on one of more of these characteristics, as the company decides that functionality, reliability, aesthetics, or price-competitiveness are the key elements of its strategy. However, at the core of every successful product there is a common element, and that is the customer.

A product is more than just the physical thing we make, or an app we build, or a service we provide. Customers have aspirations, needs, and emotions. They buy a product to solve these needs or achieve a goal. Product managers understand this and create products that deliver a customer experience that edifies their customers.

I propose this definition of a product:

*A product is the aggregate of tangible and intangible attributes that deliver benefits to the customer and solve a specific need.*

**Tangible attributes:** what your customers can use and do with your product, the set of features, technical characteristics, the ingredients of your product

**Intangible attributes:** what your customers feel and enjoy when using your product, its emotional attributes, brand value, perceived quality, security, and customer support

Rarely a set of features is enough to deliver the full customer experience, as this depends on having intangible attributes that strongly identify with your product. For example, brand recognition and values (what your company stands for), the level of security and customer support (real or perceived) that your product offers, the network of partners, and the reliability of your product's experience (to remove anxiety and provide a comfort zone to your customers). All these attributes together define a product that not only works, but is also enjoyable, trustworthy, or just simply cool. They deliver a customer experience that lets your product stand out.

Great chefs take this to heart: not only do they use high-quality ingredients to prepare their food, but they also craft their recipes in an artful presentation and offer their guests an enjoyable ambience. Just putting together good ingredients is not enough: it's how they prepare the food, present it, and serve it that delivers a unique experience to their customers.

Therefore, when you think about your product you should not look at just a bundle of features. You should consider the aggregate of tangible and intangible attributes that define the entire customer experience you provide. How are customers going to buy it? How are they going to bring it home? How are they going to use it? How are they going to get help from you?

We are surrounded by products that not only have achieved great market success, but have also redefined complete industries. Apple launched the mobile app revolution with the iPhone; Uber has single-handedly shaken the taxi industry; Waze has rendered the traditional hand-held GPS obsolete by using real time traffic information from its users, on your phone, anywhere in the world; Tesla has not only made electric cars available to anyone in the market (as long as you can afford its hefty price tag!) but has also created a network of recharging stations and introduced home batteries; and Amazon, among other things, has disrupted the traditional server housing market with its cloud-based AWS service.

Great products are those that put the customer experience at the core of their development efforts. It's by keeping a focus on customer needs and delights throughout the product development process — from discovery through delivery — that companies can create products that customers love.

# THE ROLE OF THE PRODUCT MANAGER

The product manager is often considered the CEO of the product, as they define the strategy and the vision and drive the execution of a product. This person usually leads a cross-functional team that is responsible for an entire product or product line from conception to launch.

The product manager:

- Is responsible for working with business stakeholders and partners to understand business goals and market opportunities
- Interacts with customers to understand customer needs and convert them into possible solutions
- Leads ideation, prototyping, customer validation activities aimed at creating a new product
- Manages, refines and prioritizes the product backlog
- Is responsible for launching a product into the marketplace, measuring performance, and ultimately ensuring the success of the product
- Shepherds the product through the 5 Dimensions from Discovery through Delivery in rapid iterations

In simple ways, the product manager is the person responsible for defining the "why", the "what", and the "when" of the product. These are the key decisions the product manager needs to make.

The "how" a product is built is usually a decision left to the technology team or undertaken together by its members. Product managers who have a strong "T" dimension (Technology, see HBT dimensions below) often prefer to take an active role in planning the execution together with the team. Others may leave technical decisions to their technology team. There is no right or wrong approach here, if the product manager maintains their focus on the responsibilities (the "why", the "what" and the "when" of a product) and empowers the team for the "how".

The original Apollo flight mission control room at NASA

I like to compare the product manager to a Flight Director at NASA's mission control. The flight director is responsible for the success of a space mission from start to finish. They have a team of cross-functional, highly specialized individuals, each responsible for their own practice. Each one manages a small yet complex piece of the overall mission: the engines, the communications, the astronauts' well-being, or the media relations with the outside world. Each team member is key to the mission's outcome, but only by working together as a team can the mission be carried out successfully. The flight director is ultimately responsible for the success of the mission (or its failure) but it is their team that performs the work. The flight director acts as a servant leader, trusting their team members and enabling them to take the opportune actions they need to take.

# CHARACTERISTICS OF A GREAT PRODUCT MANAGER

I find product management exciting because I consider this role to be at the intersection of science and art. It relies on business analysis, data, and research to make decisions, and it requires creativity to solve problems and devise innovative solutions. It's a role that leverages the power of both the left and the right sides of the brain. It provides challenges, excitement, innovation. And it requires entrepreneurship, creativity, and problem-solving. Great product managers demonstrate a set of skills that includes:

## Entrepreneurship

Entrepreneurship is the ability to make decisions and create things in the context of limited resources, limited information, or limited support.

## Leadership

Leadership is a combination of skills and character traits that allow you to influence, inspire, and support people around you. When you act as a servant leader to your team, you create empowerment and set the conditions for them to thrive.

## Customer focus

Customer focus is the ability to understand the customer needs, expectations, and priorities, and incorporate them into a product plan.

## Ability to listen

Listening allows you to better relate to other people, understand their problem, and create an environment of learning. As the old saying goes, "No learning comes from an open mouth."

## Empathy

Empathy is at the core of customer focus. To be able to understand your customer's needs you need to develop empathy for their problems, shift your perspective to your customer's experience, and translate your product plan into a solution that delivers benefits and delights your customers.

## Mastery of techniques

Continuous learning — from customers, from the business, from the development team, from other product managers — is key to develop mastery of techniques. These include tools, know-how, and methodologies that span across all three H-B-T dimensions.

## THE HBT DIMENSIONS

Successful product managers need to balance the three dimensions of Human, Business, and Technology. This model is a powerful guide to understand the competencies, skillset, and attitudes that product managers must have to build great products.[1]

The product manager sits at the intersection of the H-B-T dimensions. More than being an expert in any of these dimensions, the product manager must demonstrate an attitude toward each and strike a good balance between them. Building a great product means being able to balance these three dimensions.

## Human dimension

The Human dimension focuses on customer **desirability**, usability, and human-centered design. Your solution should start from the people that use your product and clearly address their needs, pain points, and expectations. Use empathy to connect to your end users and to understand their deep needs and motivations. Make the product usable by your target users so they can get value from it. Design a solution that delights your customers, generate positive emotions, and inspires adoption.

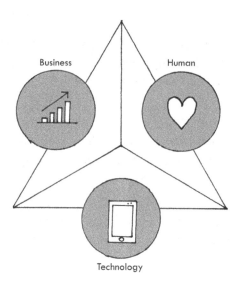

Questions you may want to answer:

- Does the product address customer wants, needs, or dreams?
- Do customers care about this product?
- Can they understand how to use it?
- Is there problem-solution fit with your product?
- Are customers happy to use your solution?

## Business dimension

The Business dimension focuses on **viability** for the business, your market, and your customers. Build the right product, at the right time, for your business and for your customers. Understand your space: market, industry, customer segments, competition, opportunity. Create a product that is valuable for your business and that customers are willing to pay for.

Questions you may want to answer:

- Is this something you should do?
- Can you validate the concept quickly before investing too much?
- Is this sustainable in the long run? Does it make financial sense?
- Do you have, or can you find, all the necessary resources to carry this forward (finance, marketing, training, support, partnerships, etc.)?
- Does it generate value, for your business, for your customers, and for your partners?
- Is there market-solution fit with your product?

## Technology dimension

The Technology dimension focuses on **feasibility**, features, performance. Employ the technology, people, and know-how to build your product. Address constraints and solve impediments. Find out creative ways to overcome problems or complexities.

Questions you may want to answer:

- Can your team build it? Is it feasible?
- What do you need to build it? (technology, processes, know-how)
- Can you slice the product in multiple releases to deliver the highest value first?
- What tradeoffs do you need to make to build the product in a reasonable timeframe?

The product manager, as the person ultimately responsible for the success of their product, acts as the glue between the team members and relies on them for broadening their expertise. After all, great products are never created in a vacuum, but are usually the result of team collaboration.

Depending on the specific experience or background of the product managers, they can get help to balance the H-B-T dimensions from their team members:

Interaction designers and researchers can support the product manager in exploring the H dimension, discovering deep human needs with empathy research and designing a usable solution that delights customers.

Engineers and developers can provide the support they need to understand the feasibility of a solution, define technological constraints, and find solutions to impediments (the T dimension).

This is often called the **product triad**: product manager, designer, and tech lead. A strong collaboration between these three roles fosters a deeper understanding of the H-B-T dimensions and the development of better products.

## A ROLE IN EVOLUTION

The role of the product manager takes different forms depending on the company, the industry, or even the types of goods or services the company produces. The most innovative companies around the globe have a formal product management role and dedicated teams to manage their products. Other companies may not have a formal product role, but rely on their technology, project, sales, or marketing teams to identify opportunities and build new products.

Traditionally, companies have delegated the responsibility for product management to either their marketing or technology departments, and the product manager role to either a brand manager, a business analyst, or a project manager. Only in the last decade or so, the role of the product manager has started to take a form in and of itself, separating from brand or project management.

Only about a third of companies in the US have clearly defined the role of product management and are mastering their product innovation pipeline: think of Google, Apple, Capital One, Adobe, Uber, Amazon. The others are either somewhere during the formalizing of this role or have yet to begin their product management journey.[2]

All this to say that the practice of product management, although not new, is evolving and is gaining stronger recognition. Training classes and certification exams are available at different competency levels to master product management skills and keep updated with the latest methodologies.

These are some good books that discuss the role of a product manager:

Steven Haines, *Managing Product Management: Empowering Your Organization to Produce Competitive Products and Brands*, McGraw-Hill Education, 2011

Marty Cagan, *Inspired: How to Create Products Customers Love*, SVPG Press, 2008

# THE THREE PILLARS OF GREAT PRODUCTS

In organizations that have developed a strong product culture, the product managers are often the driving force of innovation, the champions of customer experience, and the masters of agility. They have built their expertise on the three pillars of great products and strive to implement the three pillars as fundamental blocks of the product culture in their organization.

If your organization is still embarking on a journey to become more product-centric, starting from the three pillars will help you build the right foundation.

The next section is dedicated to the three pillars of Customer Focus, Culture of Agility, and Team Empowerment.

# REFERENCES

1.  The H-B-T model for product managers is inspired by IDEO's model of Feasibility, Desirability and Viability for new products https://www.ideou.com/blogs/inspiration/how-to-prototype-a-new-business and is widely adopted in the hiring process of new product managers at companies like Capital One and others.

2.  Steven Haines, *Managing Product Management: Empowering Your Organization to Produce Competitive Products and Brands*, McGraw-Hill, 2011.

# [PART 2]

# THE THREE PILLARS
# OF PRODUCT SUCCESS

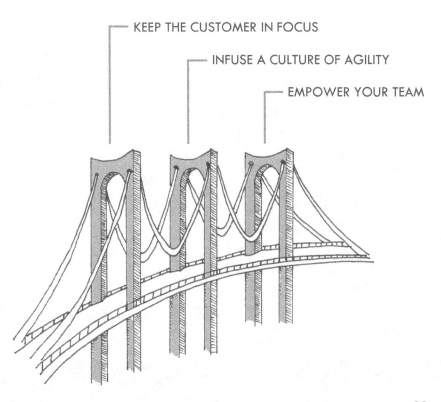

KEEP THE CUSTOMER IN FOCUS

INFUSE A CULTURE OF AGILITY

EMPOWER YOUR TEAM

Storyboards help understand the customer's journey

# [3]

# KEEP THE CUSTOMER IN FOCUS

Having a customer focus means placing the users of your product and other important stakeholders at the center of the design and development process. Customer focus requires the ability to understand the customer's needs, expectations, and priorities, and to incorporate the customer's feedback at every step of the product development process. It is probably the most important characteristic of a great product manager. After all, if you deliver a product that your customers don't like, your venture in product development may be short-lived. The customer is not only the one buying your product but is also the reason why you build it in the first place, the one choosing your product over other options, and the one who can fire your product when it is no longer needed.

*"There is only one boss. The customer. And he can fire everybody in the company from the chairman on down, simply by spending his money somewhere else."* – Sam Walton, founder of Walmart, the largest retailer in the world.

# UNDERSTAND WHO YOUR CUSTOMERS ARE AND WHAT THEY NEED

I'm an advisor in a business incubator near Washington, DC, helping new entrepreneurs launch their startup companies. Sometimes they come to me late in the process, with a product that they have already built, and ask for help in marketing their product and finding customers. They became so enamored with their product idea that they focused all their energy in building it rather than understanding who their customer really is. By the time the product is ready for launch, they have yet to determine who's going to buy it and whether customers are interested in it.

These products are affected by the Delivery Gap (see Chapter 11: Deliver). The Delivery Gap exists when products are deployed to the market without a clear understanding of how they are going to deliver benefits to customers. Closing the Delivery Gap is essential for a successful product launch, and it starts with a deeper understanding of customers and their needs.

Customer focus is about understanding who your customers are and what they need. Incorporate your users in the research and design process to make sure you create a solution that they are interested in. But don't just rely on them to tell you how to solve a problem — people can often very clearly express a problem they have, but they may not be the best ones at creating a solution for it. Steve Jobs famously said that he didn't like customer research because *"customers don't know what they want"*. That still doesn't mean you should not know who your customers are and what they need. The job of a product manager is to understand the customer needs and expectations, and then translate them into possible solutions.

## THE RIGHT CUSTOMER

You cannot build the right product unless you know who the customer is. Before your product becomes mass-market and appeals to a large segment of the population, you should start from a narrow segment of customers whose needs you understand very well. Design your solution for these customers, who will also be your early adopters.

In studying your target customers, don't look at just your "average Joe" customer, but rather find the outliers, the people who exhibit extreme behavior. Find people who feel the strongest need for your product or service, or who have the biggest pain point, or who show the weirdest way to solve their problem. These "extreme users" can reveal deeper insights into how your product or service can solve customer problems and can help you uncover opportunities you may not be aware of. In essence, study the extreme users, then design your product or service for your target customers.

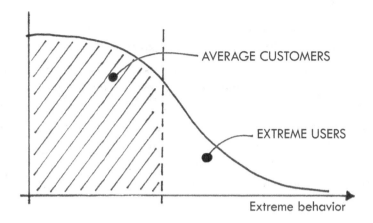

We can learn a lot more from customers who demonstrate
extreme behaviors or needs

## FOCUS ON YOUR CUSTOMERS ALL THE TIME, NOT JUST AT THE BEGINNING OR END

Customer focus is not an activity you can do solely during exploration of a new idea and then never again. Having a customer focus defines the product manager's attitude of seeking and incorporating the customer's input into your decisions at every step in the product development cycle.

Customer focus is often a synonym for Human-Centered Design, an approach to problem solving that incorporates the user feedback throughout the various stages of development of a new product or service. Designers analyze and define how customers are likely to use a product, and also validate their initial assumptions with regard to user behavior with real world tests and actual users. The customer input is sought at various stages throughout the development process, and the solution is built incrementally around how users can, want, or need to use the product, rather than forcing the users to modify their behavior to accommodate it.

The 5 Dimensions framework of product management helps to maintain customer focus at every step of product development, from Discovery to Delivery. By testing early and often, you maintain alignment between your business objectives and your customer expectations and can adjust your plan if needed. You also learn what drives your customer's desire to adopt your solution and can use this information to plan your product launch, marketing campaigns, and customer support activities.

Here are some quick tips:

## TIPS

- When you start a new product, talk to customers to develop an understanding of their perspective and quickly validate your initial concepts.
- Seek and incorporate customer feedback at every step in the development phase. Test every new prototype and key product decisions with customers or end users.
- During the first five to 10 weeks, spend most of your time on discovery and validation, rather than on development. Then continue incorporating customer feedback at regular intervals.
- Repeat each test with multiple customers to find overall patterns or outliers in behavior.
- Prefer face-to-face interactions. Observe how customers actually use your product (including prototype testing) rather than just asking their opinions.

# INVEST IN YOUR CUSTOMER EXPERIENCE

Customer experience is an essential part of a great product. Customers are not buying your product because of its features —they are buying it because it solves a need and delivers a user experience they want. When you build a product that customers love and are delighted to use, they become loyal ambassadors of your brand. You have delivered a great product that customers love.

The customer experience looks at the broader interaction of a customer with a particular organization, usually over the duration of their relationship. What drove that person to choose this product? What job did that person hire the product to do? How has the customer interacted with the organization after the initial use of the product?

The experience your product or service delivers can drive strong responses in adoption or rejection of a product or service: *"Thirty-nine percent of new customers switch financial institution after the first negative experience"* - Jeff Dennes - Chief Digital Officer, BBVA @ BAI Retail 2015

The customer experience extends beyond the use of a product and includes brand relationship (including emotional connection with your brand and what it represents) and interactions across all touchpoints (channels, physical and digital touchpoints, support, partners). When building a product (or service), it's important to think about the overall customer experience and not just a set of features in your product. Fortunately, there are several tools that help product managers understand the customer needs, validate prototypes, and build the right product. I'll discuss these tools in the Discover, Design, and Develop chapters.

The examples below have one characteristic in common: they have redefined the customer experience for their category. It is this extremely focused attention to the customer experience that distinguishes successful products from mediocre ones.

## SOUTHWEST AIRLINES

Southwest, one of the most respected and successful airlines in history, has been profitable for more than 40 consecutive years, quite a rare achievement in the airline industry.[1] The company has brought a series of operational efficiencies to the system, simplifying the management of the airline and reducing costs. For example, since airlines make money when their planes are in the air, one of the company's key metrics is the turnaround time at the gate (the shorter the time, the faster the plane can fly off to a new destination); Southwest aircrafts fly an average of nearly six flights or about 11 hours per day.

Besides the operational efficiencies that have been studied and copied by other airlines around the world, what makes Southwest stand out to the competition is their strong customer-centric focus. So much so that their stock ticker symbol is LUV, short for "Love". It is a single word that summarizes the focus on customer experience and satisfaction.

The company's motto is "Be nice", a commitment to deliver excellent customer service in any situation. Southwest employees are selected and trained to deliver on this promise.

*"In 2014, the airline proudly unveiled a bold new look: Heart. The new aircraft livery, airport experience, and logo showcase the dedication of Southwest Employees to connect Customers with what's important in their lives."* - Southwest Corporate fact sheet.[2]

## UBER

Uber has reinvented the ride-sharing industry and is threatening the century-old taxi industry in many countries around the world. Taxi apps existed long before Uber. You could use them to book a taxi and wait for it to arrive. Uber made the entire process smoother (just pick your location on a map and the system finds the closest car for you) and on-demand (call a ride right when and where you need it, no need to book it in advance or find a taxi stand).

The previous taxi apps brought existing service models to the user's phone, without really changing the overall customer experience. Uber didn't just build a ride reservation app, it took the opportunity to solve a few unmet needs that traditional taxi apps didn't solve, redefining the customer experience and setting a higher standard for everyone.

- Uber cars come to you based on your GPS location at the time that you need it. No need for competition with other passengers, or to make a reservation. The service finds a car ride where and when you require it.

- With Uber, you can monitor the driver's progress on a map and see where they are at any time during the trip. It makes you feel reassured that you are being serviced, and you know how long to wait.

Uber, like many other companies, adopted Agile and Human-Centered Design concepts from the beginning. It did not try to be all things to everyone. It built a Minimum Viable Product (MVP) with only a limited set of features deemed important for validating its new concept. At first, it launched in the local San Francisco market, limiting the variability associated to multiple markets and the marketing costs. And it focused only on one type of service (black cars). It validated the core principles of its model, and then expanded to the other cities and built additional features in the product.

Uber is a great example of iterative and adaptive development of a new product, and of keeping a strong focus on the customers and their needs. To its product managers, Uber *"demands passion for the customer, great technical depth, principled thinking, well-honed product judgment, a stubborn refusal to settle, bold innovation, a high design bar and a mentality of starting with the customer first and working backwards."*[3]

# DESIGN THINKING

Design Thinking is a design process that has surged to prominence because it allows teams to research and design solutions to customer problems that are difficult to analyze or define. It offers an iterative cycle of ideation and validation, whose goal is to design solutions that meet customers' needs. It works best in the white space of product innovation where a clear solution is not available and, sometimes, the customer problem may not be fully defined. By incorporating elements of human-centered design, Design Thinking offers multiple opportunities to validate ideas and solutions with customers and correct the path if necessary.

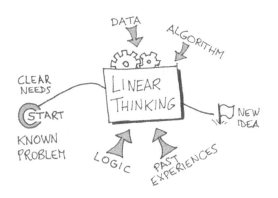

IDEO, the design firm that is widely recognized as having brought Design Thinking to prominence, provides this definition: *"Design thinking is a process for creative problem solving. Design thinking utilizes elements from the designer's toolkit like empathy and experimentation to arrive at innovative solutions."*[4]

## LINEAR VERSUS CREATIVE THINKING

When needs and problems are well-defined, we humans have an innate ability to use linear thinking to find the best solutions. By applying logic and past experiences, we follow a linear process from problem to solution.

Real innovation often happens in the "white space". This is the open, undiscovered space where exploration and discovery are essential activities to define the problem we are trying to solve or identify a new opportunity. When the problem space is not fully understood, or the customer need is not clear, linear thinking offers very little help. We need a different process, one that fosters creative thinking and allows us to develop a new understanding of the problem space. Design Thinking leverages creative thinking and helps us work on fuzzy, difficult, poorly defined problems, also called "wicked problems".

Discovery is the essential activity at the beginning of the product design process that focuses on understanding the

customer's needs and defining the problem space. In Design Thinking we use several methods to observe and build empathy with the users, connect with them on an emotional level, and learn about them as individuals and their needs. This deeper understanding of their values, beliefs, and motivations allows for ideating solutions that are both a better fit and less obvious. By incorporating customer feedback at multiple steps in the process, we can validate the solutions and correct the path if necessary.

## THE FIVE PHASES OF DESIGN THINKING

Design Thinking is often represented as an iterative cycle through a series of phases. These are not necessarily linear as the cycle can be interrupted and repeated at any moment as needed. The basic idea is that each phase offers a specific goal in the process of discovering and designing a new solution.

The Design Thinking process is an alternate of:

- FLARE: looking for new ideas, learning, creating, discovering
- FOCUS: analyzing the ideas, synthesizing the insights, and validating the best solutions

Design Thinking enables you to go beyond the initial idea or predefined requirements and discover a broader set of opportunities and solutions. It allows teams to explore new ideas, get out of their comfort zones, and avoid sticking to preconceived solutions.

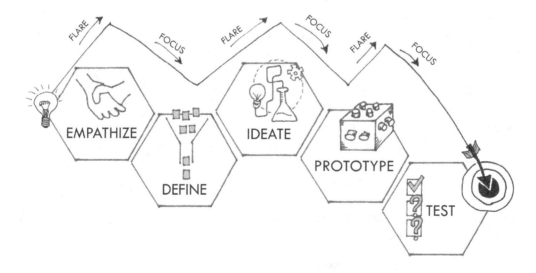

The flare-focus cycle of Design Thinking[5]

There are a variety of tools to use in each of the Design Thinking stages. The choice of the tools is up to you and the context you operate in. I describe many of these tools in the Discovery and Design chapters, and the following is just a brief description of each phase.

| | EMPHATIZE | DEFINE | IDEATE | PROTOTYPE | TEST |
|---|---|---|---|---|---|
| **TYPE OF ACTIVITY** | Flare out, learn, generate insights | Focus, select insights | Flare out then focus, generate ideas | Flare out, design solutions | Focus, select solution |
| **FOCUS ON** | Quantity, not quality | Problem statements, patterns, key insights | Quantity of ideas, variety, unexplored connections | Desirability of one or more solutions | Validation of solution, customer feedback |
| **KEY ATTITUDE** | Empathy<br>Observation<br>Listening<br>Non-judgmental | Analysis<br>Collaboration | Creativity<br>Non-judgmental<br>Building upon each other's ideas | Creativity<br>Exploration<br>Solve the customer's need | Observation<br>Analysis<br>Collaboration<br>Listening |

## EMPATHIZE with your customers

Connect with your customers on an emotional level to discover and understand their deeper needs. Explore not only what they do and need, but also the "why", the deeper reasons that inspire them to act that way.

Often, customers perceive a need and are eager to discuss a solution. But their solution may not be what they really need. Instead, look for the deeper motivations: what brings your customers to think about that problem, what are they trying to solve for? It's this deeper exploration of customer needs and aspirations that allows your team to discover better ideas.

| | |
|---|---|
| **Focus on:** | Quantity, unexpected behaviors, extreme needs |
| **Key attitude:** | Observe, listen, inquire, explore, defer judgment, keep an open mind |
| **What tools to use:** | Empathy interviews, observations, secondary research, market exploration, Customer Journey Maps |

## DEFINE the problem

Synthesize the insights, the data, and the observations you collected and identify key problems and needs. Look for common traits, as well as for contradictions. Define one or more problem statements to solve for.

| | |
|---|---|
| **Focus on:** | Data, insights, observations, contradictions |
| **Key attitude:** | Analyze, collaborate |
| **What tools to use:** | Mindmap, synthesis of research, user profiles, insight generation, Customer Journey Map, problem statement definition |

## IDEATE solutions

This is the phase dedicated to generating ideas and solutions. Focus on the problem statement(s) you are trying to solve for and generate as many ideas as possible. Think about ways to solve the problem outside the obvious. Brainstorm with your team and build on each other's ideas.

The goal is to generate as many ideas as possible. This is the time to hold back judgment and have a license to be crazy. Some ideas may seem impossible, others completely outside of your comfort zone. Keep building your idea list.

| | |
|---|---|
| **Focus on:** | Quantity first, then quality |
| **Key attitude:** | Ideate, defer judgment, build upon each other's ideas, think outside the box |
| **What tools to use:** | Group brainstorming, storyboarding, sketching, idea ranking and selection, creative prompts |

## PROTOTYPE possible solutions

This is the phase that brings your ideas to life. Select one (or more) idea(s) and build a prototype. This can take several forms, and it's up to you and your team to decide the best way to build the prototype. The goal is to do it with minimal investment (of time, resources, money). Most likely, you are going to iterate on multiple cycles of Prototype and Test, so getting started as quickly as possible is certainly an advantage.

You may even decide to build more than one prototype, especially if you have multiple ideas or you are still undecided on which may be the best solution. Prototypes serve to test your ideas with customers and understand what works.

| | |
|---|---|
| **Focus on:** | Key hypotheses, user experience, desirability |
| **Key attitude:** | Create, build, learn, validate |

**What tools to use**: Physical/digital prototyping, experience prototyping, define hypotheses and assumptions, MVP

## TEST and validate with your customers

The Test phase is about validating your ideas with customers and learning what works and what doesn't. Test the prototype with your customers and validate whether they are happy to use it. Learn if your solution solves their needs and identify any changes needed. Then incorporate the feedback and start another cycle of prototyping until you are certain the solution you have created fully addresses the customer needs and delivers the expected user experience.

**Focus on**: Validation and learning from your customers, measure success

**Key attitude**: Learn, analyze, listen, observe, ask, openness to failure

**What tools to use**: Prototype testing, empathy interviews, observations, user testing

### FURTHER READING

A Google search for "Design Thinking" brings up a variety of resources to explore. Two organizations that have grown to prominence in the Design Thinking space are IDEO and the d.school at Stanford University.

**IDEO** is a design company that pioneered customer-centric methods starting in the '90s and is recognized as a forward-thinking innovator in customer experience design. The famous "shopping cart" business case has been read (or watched on video) by millions, as a cornerstone example of the practices employed by IDEO. A visit to their website and a reading of some of their stories are a great source of insights on customer-centric design techniques. IDEO University offers training classes year-round. http://www.ideou.com/pages/design-thinking-resources

**Stanford University** founded the **d.school**, a customer-centric design program whose cornerstone is a Design Thinking curriculum with hands-on experience. Many product leaders have attended the program and earned their d.school certification. Its website also offers a variety of resources to learn more on Design Thinking and become familiar with the different techniques. http://dschool.stanford.edu/

# REFERENCES

1.  Source: http://seekingalpha.com/article/1312991-southwest-airlines-40-consecutive-years-of-profits - Retrieved Nov 30, 2016 - Seeking Alpha - "Southwest Airlines: 40 Consecutive Years of Profits"

2.  Southwest Corporate Fact Sheet - http://www.swamedia.com/channels/Corporate-Fact-Sheet/pages/corporate-fact-sheet - Retrieved Nov 30, 2016

3.  Source Uber: Job description for "Product Manager - Customer Relationships - Customer Obsession" https://www.uber.com/careers/list/19578/?mode=job&iis=joindot-V101A-pmgmt - Retrieved Nov 30, 2016

4.  From IDEO's website https://www.ideou.com/pages/design-thinking - Retrieved July 31, 2018

5.  Adapted from the Design Thinking framework at Stanford University http://dschool.stanford.edu/

# NOTES

Agile transformations start with a change of mindset and values

# [4]

# INFUSE A CULTURE OF AGILITY

Today's market is increasingly more competitive as new products are launched daily and entire industries are thrown upside down by innovators. Think of Uber and Lyft, how they have revolutionized the taxi industry, which — caught by surprise — is struggling to redefine its identity and maintain market relevance. Or the recent purchase of Whole Foods by Amazon, the leader of online sales which is increasingly moving into the brick-and-mortar retail space, threatening long-held leaders in this market.

Companies today cannot afford to ideate, research, and develop a new product over a long time. The risk is that by the time the product is ready for launch, someone nimbler, faster, more agile, who can identify an opportunity and quickly bring a solution to life, has already taken the top spot in the market.

Toyota realized this in the '60s. American car companies at the time had market dominance in the US: General Motors, Ford, and Chrysler in 1965 commanded a total of 90.6% of the US market.[1] They were, by far, the gorillas, and nothing seemed to threaten that dominance. Until a few engineers at Toyota grew concerned with the inefficiencies in their manufacturing chain and started introducing innovations.

The first such innovation was a process called Kanban (Japanese for "billboard"). In its simple form, Kanban imposes a Work in Progress (WIP) limit, thereby reducing the number of items that can be worked on at a given time. With only a limited number of working slots, a new activity can begin only when a previous task is completed and its slot becomes available. With smaller batches and a lower WIP limit, Kanban increases the flow of work through the system.

The Toyota engineers also established a feedback loop for their production process. If a problem was spotted, or an improvement could be suggested, the workers stopped the manufacturing process immediately, raised the concern with their supervisor, and worked out a solution. The manufacturing work resumed only after the problem was fixed or a solution was found. This drove quality improvements for both the final product and the production environment.

These and other innovations created a culture of continuous improvement and cross-functional team empowerment that propelled Toyota's production system to higher productivity and higher quality than any of their American counterparts. (Fast forward 50 years and Toyota is, today, the largest automaker in the world, ahead of GM and even Volkswagen).[2]

## FURTHER READING

https://www.scruminc.com/takeuchi-and-nonaka-roots-of-scrum/

https://en.wikipedia.org/wiki/Kanban

# MOVING AT THE SPEED OF INNOVATION

A few guys in the IT industry started wondering if the efficiency principles that Toyota had pioneered could be applied to the software development industry. Jeff Sutherland and Ken Schwaber presented an original application of these principles at a Texas conference in 1995. They dubbed the process "Scrum", from the game of rugby describing where a group of players gets the ball and needs to advance it to score the point. The team self-organizes and identifies the best way to proceed based on the actual situation on the field (and the tactics of the competing team) rather than pre-imposed rules and positions. This concept reflects the adaptability and cross-functional nature of Scrum. Today, Scrum is one of the most adopted Agile frameworks around the world.

If the Toyota story teaches us something, it is that market dominance is not a guarantee for future success. An incumbent can be displaced by a disruptor in a matter of years, sometimes in a matter of months.

Blackberry invented the smartphone, destroying established competitors like Nokia and Motorola who were unprepared for the market shift brought forward by Blackberry's innovations.

## FURTHER READING

"How Blackberry fell", The New Yorker, August 12, 2013
http://www.newyorker.com/tech/elements/how-blackberry-fell

Then, when Apple introduced the iPhone in 2007, Blackberry was itself taken by surprise and lost more than 50% in market value in less than two years.[3] It was not able to stop a shift in customer preferences (Blackberry now has less than 0.1% of the global market share).[4]

The cost of starting an online business today is small compared to what it was just 10 or 15 years ago. Today you don't need to pay large amounts of money upfront for a server or software. Using the cloud, open-source software, and widely available Software-as-a-Service (SaaS) tools, online businesses can be started in days or weeks, instead of months, at a fraction of the cost.

This means that the speed at which innovations and new business models are created has increased exponentially. Just a look at the number of apps available on the app stores of Apple and Google Android is staggering: as of 2016 there were more than 4 million apps available for download.[5] The number of apps keeps increasing.[6]

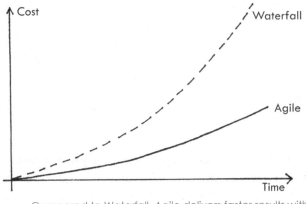

Compared to Waterfall, Agile delivers faster results with lower cost of change

Successful companies today adopt Agile practices throughout their organizations. Agile allows them to move fast, adapt to changing market conditions, and validate new ideas in a limited time. Coupled with the ease and speed at which new technology can be built, and with a customer-centric focus on user needs, these companies can deliver benefits and value to their customers faster, and reduce their risk exposure tremendously.

Because Agile employs an iterative process, it minimizes rework and allows teams to validate their work with customers and stakeholders at multiple times during the development process. Compared to Waterfall approaches to software development, Agile methodologies deliver faster outcomes, with less effort and higher customer satisfaction.

# BEING AGILE VS DOING AGILE

"Doing Agile" means adopting and implementing Agile methodologies, ensuring the development team follows Agile principles. By properly implementing these methodologies, teams can leverage increased transparency, communication and flexibility, thereby reducing the risks associated with building the wrong product, and creating stronger alignment among the organization and its customers.

However, even the best-intended efforts of adopting Agile often fall into the trap of the traditional mode of seeing Agile practices limited to the development team. The entire product development pipeline is a sequence of Waterfall phases until the development phase begins — product innovation, requirements and design are treated as sequential steps in Waterfall and often fully analyzed in great details before moving to the next phase. At the development phase, Agile methodologies are employed to create the end product. And any subsequent activities of market launch and validation are also Waterfall.

IDEATION, REQUIREMENTS, DESIGN    DEVELOPMENT    DEPLOYMENT, VALIDATION, SUPPORT
(WATERFALL)                       (AGILE)         (WATERFALL)

Because the development team is employing Agile, it gives a false impression of agility throughout the process. What is the value of using Agile in development if the process of sourcing new ideas, ideating a new product, and testing new concepts are done in Waterfall? How useful is Agile if, after you have launched a new product, you fail to connect with customers and learn from them how the product is performing and how it can be improved?

A product may be built in increments, but if it takes months to define the requirements and design a solution, by the time the finished product hits the market, it may deliver a solution that is no longer needed.

For these reasons, Agile should not be limited to development teams. Luckily for us, Agile, Design Thinking, and Lean Startup methodologies help organizations infuse agility at every step of the product innovation pipeline. By employing these methodologies, the product innovation pipeline can not only become more agile but can also be turned upside down. Ideally, an organization can strive for market validation of a new idea before even investing in building it.

## Agile

Build in iterations, one step at a time. Validate each iteration with end users. Adjust and re-prioritize as necessary.

## Design Thinking

Approach problem-solving with a customer-centric iterative approach based on learning, ideation, and prototyping.

## Lean Startup

Learn-build-measure cycle focused on early validation and MVP.

# CULTURE TRANSFORMATION AT ANY LEVEL

Adopting Agile in an environment limited to the development team while the rest of the organization marches forward using traditional methods reduces the impact of Agile and often undermines the benefits it can bring. To reap the benefits of Agile, align itself with the marketplace, and better satisfy its customers' needs, an organization should infuse a culture of agility throughout its ranks.

Agility does not need to start from the top. Often, a culture of agility is inspired from the bottom. Product managers and Scrum Masters are often in the best positions to help their organizations become more agile by acting as champions of agility — driving customer focus and building in iterations. They can demonstrate the value and enable executives to become more comfortable. But to drive adoption and align the organization around a culture of agility, executives and business leaders need to embrace it and become champions for their organizations.

In almost all situations, a successful adoption of Agile principles requires much more than just doing Agile at a team level. It requires adopting a culture of agility across the organization and at all levels. It requires "being" Agile, rather than just "doing" Agile.

Business leaders should adopt the key principles and accept the iterative development model offered by Agile to reduce risk, optimize return, and satisfy customer needs. Executives need to feel comfortable with a (relative) lack of long-term plans, and instead accept that roadmaps are designed to provide a short-term view and may change dramatically over time. At their core Agile methodologies are designed to control risk. Isn't this one of the most important tenets of any business? Agile provides transparency into the work, shortens the feedback loop with customers enabling rapid validation of new business ideas, and improves productivity by better employing the available resources and removing impediments.

Business leaders should appreciate the value of launching an MVP (Minimum Viable Product) in the marketplace as early as possible, learning from their customers, validating (or invalidating) hypotheses, and improving from it. Executives should empower their teams to make decisions and self-organize how they work, letting go of control and delegating authority to prioritize product development.

## REDUCE THE COST OF CHANGE

For organizations that build products there are many risks. But among the biggest is the risk of spending a lot of time and a ton of money in building the most innovative, coolest, hottest new tool, and then seeing it fail in the marketplace. Usually, this is the result of one of more of the following:

- Failure to align with customer needs or changing customer needs
- Lack of support from management
- Timeframe extended too far, delay in getting to market
- Poor choice of technology, processes, or tools
- Poor communication among key stakeholders
- Lack of quality or poor quality processes

By empowering teams to work across multi-disciplinary boundaries, by fostering a culture of communication and transparency, and by allowing teams to build software in rapid increments, Agile reduces the impact of these issues and the risk of failure.

At the core of Agile are collaboration among team members, transparency of information, and flexibility in planning. As stated in the Agile Manifesto, Agile does not intend to replace the good practices of logging documentation, planning, or following processes. Its aim is, instead, to move the focus to people, their interactions, and the development of a "working" product.[7]

Over time, Agile has been adopted in organizations that work in areas other than software development. Departments as diverse as Legal, HR, Business Analysis, and Marketing are adopting Agile to streamline their processes and maintaining closer visibility of deliverables. The adoption of Agile in these departments often results in significant performance improvements. It also creates stronger synergy in cross-functional teams, and allows the entire organization to move with agility, rather than in mixed steps of Agile and Waterfall.

For more information, there are many books on the topic. For a quick read, Wikipedia offers a descriptive and extensive explanation of the Agile methodology.

FURTHER READING

"Agile software development", Wikipedia
https://en.wikipedia.org/wiki/Agile_software_development

## CREATE TRANSPARENCY ACROSS THE ORGANIZATION

Development teams don't live in a void. They live in a complex ecosystem with many stakeholders, including management, partners, and customers. Transparency, as a key principle of Agile, ensures that all stakeholders are informed, aligned, and updated on the project at every possible juncture. When everybody works together and shares information about their work with everyone else, teams can perform better and reduce the risks involved in building something new or untested.

Transparency is achieved in multiple ways:

- By creating visibility of the work and processes used by the team using Backlogs, User Stories, Kanban boards and other artifacts. Key information about the work the team needs to do, its order and priorities, and how everything fits together is available to everyone to see at any time.
- A prioritized Backlog or Product Journey Map shows everyone what are the highest priorities the team needs to tackle.
- Scrum events offer a planned, timeboxed, collaborative way to share updates with stakeholders and receive feedback.
- Rapid prototyping, development, and user testing allow for collection of

feedback from customers and end users. The development team receives frequent feedback and iterates as necessary.

- Cross-functional teams that allow multiple departments (IT Operations, Marketing, Customer Support, etc.) to be informed of major milestones and deadlines and work together to create the end product.

## FOSTER COLLABORATION AMONG TEAM MEMBERS

A key tenant of the Agile Manifesto is the interaction among people. Teams are multi-disciplinary and self-organizing. Collaboration ensures the proper flow of information, the surfacing of any issues, and the collaborative effort in trying to solve impediments.

Collaboration has shown to:

- Create accountability: Once you have shared your ideas with someone else, they are likely to have a vested interest in its success. After all, the team's success is everyone's success.

- Multiply success: The old saying goes *"Two heads are better than one."* More people working together generate more ideas and can see the same problem from different angles.

- Increase participation in your project: When you invite others to contribute, they feel valued as their opinion is heard. They become your fans, and support you when needed.

- Define the non-negotiables: By working with others on your team you are more likely to identify and negotiate a set of constraints that cannot be removed. These are the non-negotiables, or the must-haves of the project.

## FLEXIBILITY IN PLANS AND ADAPTABILITY TO CHANGE

No plan is ever set in stone. As much as architects and engineers strive to design every single detail of a new house and craft precise blueprints, there is always something that needs to change when the construction takes place. It could be an old tree the city doesn't allow to be cut from the property, a heavy storm that hits unexpectedly and causes delays, or your mother-in-law who suggests a new color for the kitchen's floor tiles. Whenever change happens, you need to change the blueprints, extend the construction timeframe, or return the tiles to get the new color. If you stick with your original plan allowing for no changes, you could end up with problems with the city, being dissatisfied with the closing date, or an unhappy mother-in-law.

Whatever the reason, you are better off when you embrace mechanisms to adapt to changing conditions, needs, or markets. Teams encounter impediments all the time. They need to have the flexibility to modify their plans and find workarounds.

Flexibility means not only adaptability to unforeseen events, but also to the prospect of not being able to plan everything upfront. When you set a hard deadline and then work your way back to hit that deadline, you are not incorporating flexibility in your system to allow for changes or unforeseen events. When you set a deadline and do not allow for flexibility of scope, you set the conditions for either poor quality of the end product or a ramp-up in costs (and, often, missing the deadline too). Plans and deadlines in Agile are important, but they are achieved because of work being completed, and scope being adjusted.

## ABILITY TO FAIL AND LEARN

The ability to fail and learn is important to create the conditions for an Agile culture change to flourish.

*"I have not failed. I've just found 10,000 ways that won't work."*

- Thomas A. Edison

As important as adopting Agile is, so is creating a culture that allows teams to experiment and fail. Treating failure as a learning opportunity can be very powerful. Teams can learn a lot from failure. It can help them discover new ways of doing things, new features customers want, or simply avoid further investments toward a path that has proven unsuccessful.

*"Change and uncertainty are part of life. Our job is not to resist them but to build the capability to recover when unexpected events occur. If you don't always try to uncover what is unseen and understand its nature, you will be ill prepared to lead."* - Ed Catmull

More important than allowing a team to fail is allowing the team to learn from failure, correct itself, and grow.

A culture that supports failure as a learning opportunity also allows teams to test and validate ideas much faster. Planning is no longer seen as a need to cover all possible occurrences and protect against failure, but rather becomes a useful tool for exploration. Instead of spending months to prepare very detailed and risk-averse plans, the team can define the minimum set of hypotheses to validate and the activities to perform, and then execute, the plan.

# BEING AGILE VERSUS DOING AGILE AT CAPITAL ONE

In early 2016, I led a product team at Capital One dedicated to building new capabilities for our internal bankers. One of the key ideas was a tool that we thought would revolutionize how our bankers searched for customer information and managed their accounts. It was a gigantic effort, probably a multi-year project. But we needed to validate whether we were on the right path, and do so quickly before the next budget season started.

After a few weeks of discovery, prototype testing, and interviews, we had a (long!) list of features that we wanted to build. To make sense of it all, we created a Product Journey Map that consisted of 18 stages and seven different journeys (corresponding to the various personas that we had identified and their interactions with the system). This Product Journey Map took over an entire wall in our office, and its main benefit was to bring visibility to our entire plan, and allow the team to focus on the top priorities.

We decided to build an MVP. In fact, we identified a few core hypotheses we wanted to validate, and a limited set of features to learn from our bankers if the new system was as useful as we imagined (more on Product Journey Maps and MVPs in Chapters 7 and 8).

We started with Kanban in Sprint Zero, switched to Scrum as soon as our backlog was ready, and tested each prototype with a group of stakeholders and bankers. We kept a strong focus on the MVP, limiting its scope, and avoiding the external pressures to extend it as much as possible.

Despite working on a completely new technology stack, my team was able to go from ideation to production deployment in a little more than four months. By slicing the feature set and releasing an MVP early, we were able to verify our assumptions and get feedback from end-users, and use this data to adjust the plan. This, in turn, ensured that we could spend the rest of the budget building what customers wanted, rather than building things no one knew if they would work until the whole system was completed.[8]

As a comparison, another business unit had previously started another project based on the same technology. They had already spent months writing detailed documentation for all requirements upfront and were planning to launch the new system all at once, only when all capabilities were built. In their estimate, the development phase would take about nine months. On top of that, the top management had imposed a hard deadline on the team as it wanted to avoid renewing the license of an older system. They had basically set both the scope of the work and its schedule.

Instead of targeting an MVP, they were targeting a full system launch. By fixing the requirements early on and setting a hard deadline for launching the complete system, they had undermined one of the key advantages of using Agile: the possibility to adapt to changing requirements and user needs. The development team used Scrum, but the overall project was basically Waterfall.

Needless to say, the project went very differently than planned. When things started to become more complex than expected, causing delays in the schedule, the team couldn't adapt and change the scope. Because they were "all-in", they had to build the whole thing and deliver at once. Nine months later they were nowhere near the end of the development, and had nothing that could be released in the market. When the deadline came and the system was not ready, they had to renew the soon-to-be-useless and expensive software license.

# HOW TO START WITH AGILE

Successfully implementing Agile does not mean doing daily stand-ups with the team. At least, not only that :-)

Stand-ups are a great way to share updates and keep everyone accountable for the progress on the work, but by themselves they don't drive agility. Agility happens at several levels in the organization, and should include the three P's: People, Project, and Process.

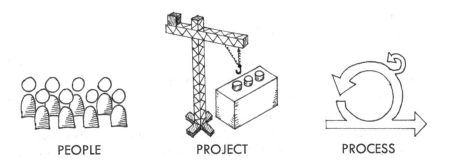

PEOPLE          PROJECT          PROCESS

## PEOPLE

People and culture are at the core of agility. You need to develop knowledge and skill set, and have the right people on the team.

- Training: Enroll your people in Agile training classes to give them the foundation to understand and implement Agile practices. There are many offerings that cover various topics and price points. The training classes offered by some organizations, including the Scrum Alliance or Scrum.org, also offer a certification exam that is widely recognized in the industry. Train your executives too — culture change comes from the top.

- Coaching: Insert an Agile coach on your team. Coaches are great at steering your team towards the right frame of mind and use of the tools, and can provide suggestions on how to apply the framework to suit your specific needs. Coaches can support both the teams and the executives for a broad culture change in the organization.

- Multi-functional team: Make sure your team is multi-functional and has all the abilities to deliver a full project. Include marketing, legal, training, sales, and other specialties as needed. Even if they are not assigned full-time, make sure the development team has access to them when needed.

- Empower your team: Self-organizing teams drive the work and adjust their processes as needed. Make sure executives leave room for the team to make its own decisions and empower the product manager to take full ownership and accountability for the priorities of the product.

## PROJECT

Starting a new project is a great time to begin using an Agile methodology like Scrum with your team. However, since the project's scope and purpose may be completely new, and the team may also come together for the first time, there is an inevitable learning curve for context, priorities, technology, and even social rules between people. Ramping up and adopting Agile practices can be an additional burden and I've found the following tips to help:

- Sprint Zero: Start your project with a Sprint Zero. During this Sprint, schedule no development work, and instead let your team focus on setting up their development environment and familiarizing themselves with the needs of the project. The team may drive and prioritize most of the Stories in Sprint Zero, and that is okay. If the team is new to Agile/Scrum, practice the Scrum ceremonies and their flow without the pressure of development work.

- Use Kanban in Sprint Zero: Adopting Kanban for Sprint Zero removes the pressure that comes from a strict timeboxed scheduling of activities in

Scrum. Use Kanban instead and let your team pick up Stories as they are Ready. Kanban offers many of the benefits of Scrum including transparency and communication. It gives time to the product manager to refine its backlog if needed. And it allows the team to discover its own flow, which can be useful when a team first comes together. You can switch to Scrum later, when your backlog is refined enough and the team is ready.

- Physical board: Start with a physical board to visualize the backlog and the work the team is doing with physical cards for each of the User Stories. The Kanban board creates the foundation for team collaboration, and allows everyone to see the flow of work and get used to the process. The product manager refines and prioritizes new work in the "Ready" column. Developers take a card and work on it through the working stages (usually, "Doing" and "Test"). When the work is completed, they move it to the "Done" column. At any given time, everyone knows what the team is working on, and what's coming next.

One common obstacle in successfully starting Scrum is having a product backlog that is refined and prioritized enough to have User Stories ready for Sprint One, and possibly for a second Sprint afterward. A few times, I started a new project and brought together a development team when my backlog was not yet ready. Because I could not provide a Sprint Backlog, we weren't able to start a proper Sprint.

Instead, we switched to Kanban. As I prepared my Stories one by one, the team picked them up and started working on them. We kept this flow going for a few weeks, until I had built enough of a backlog to start "Scrumming".

One time we had a Sprint Zero in Kanban for five weeks, and that was totally acceptable. The team used that time to become accustomed to the new technology and the project's needs, and to ramp up its productivity without the pressure of the Scrum time boxes.

## PROCESS

Starting on the right foot for Scrum (or other Agile methodology) is important, and a delicate task. The methodology is simple, its application more difficult, but there are several nuances that can make it more effective.

- Backlog: As discussed above, having a backlog of work that's properly refined and prioritized is necessary to plan the activities. A backlog is not just a list of requirements, but rather, represents a list of user needs and outcomes that your development effort should satisfy.

- Roles: Make sure to have clarity on the roles, especially the Product Owner, and the Scrum Master. Ownership and responsibilities should be clearly defined and properly delegated. Effective Product Owners drive priorities and outcomes of their product. Scrum Masters support their team in adopting Agile and becoming beacons of agility throughout the organization.

- Stand-up: The Daily Stand-up can be an effective meeting to establish transparency and accountability. Follow the tips provided in other sections of this book. Especially, ensure that the discussion in not just a mere recital of tasks completed or to-dos, but rather is centered around the work the team is doing and how to advance it towards the expected outcome.

- Customer feedback: Incorporate customer feedback at every step of the way. Sprint Reviews are excellent opportunities to validate what you have built and collect feedback from stakeholders and customers. Use Prototype testing and other Discovery techniques, periodically, to make sure everything you do is aligned to customer needs and delivers value.

# WHAT IS SCRUM

Scrum is an Agile framework for developing new products and extending existing ones. Scrum is one of the most common frameworks implemented in Agile. It has been around since the end of the 1990s, and provides a repeatable, consistent, and effective set of events to help development teams build products.

Scrum is not by itself a technique to build products, rather it provides the framework to enable teams to collaborate and follow a set of rules. Teams can then employ the specific techniques most suitable to designing and developing their products.

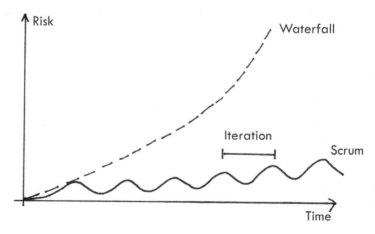

The risk of change is strongly reduced with Scrum

Scrum enables teams to build products using an iterative and adaptive process, therefore reducing risk and improving the outcome. It reduces the cost of changing and adapting the plan to varying requirements or customer needs, and therefore reduces the overall risk of the project. Work is usually done in multiple iterations of the same duration. During each iteration, the team builds a piece of the product, tests it, and collects feedback from customers and stakeholders. The team then prepares to work on the next iteration and repeats the process until the full product is completed. Because Scrum offers multiple opportunities for inspecting the work and collecting feedback, it allows teams to validate their product along the way, or quickly change course if needed.

## THREE PILLARS

Scrum upholds the three fundamental pillars of empiricism: transparency, inspection, and adaptation.

### Transparency

Scrum provides multiple opportunities for the team and its stakeholders to come together, inspect, and validate the work being done. Because the work does not happen in a black box, everyone can see what the team is doing and what to expect.

The Product Backlog is a living document that the Product Owner shares with the rest of the team and their stakeholders. Because the Backlog is visible and shared among team members and stakeholders, everyone knows what the team is working on and what's coming next. The work that the team commits to is not dictated by the Product Owner, but is negotiated with the team members. User Stories are not hard-written requirements, but rather placeholders for conversations. The team self-organizes to find the best ways to do the work and deliver the expected results.

The Sprint Review is a key moment in the Sprint timeline wherein the team has the opportunity to share the work done with stakeholders and customers, and collect their feedback. Customers and stakeholders gain visibility into the work, and the team can adjust the plan if needed.

Transparency enables stronger collaboration, promotes trust among everyone involved, and reduces the risks of rework.

### Inspection

Scrum provides multiple opportunities for inspecting both the work product and the process that the team adopts to create it. Stakeholders and customers have opportunities to participate in the development process at regular intervals and to provide feedback on the work being done. The Product Owner reviews and accepts the work as the development team completes it. And the team reviews its processes and finds ways to better work together.

By inspecting the work being done, the team creates an environment that fosters transparency and adaptation to changing conditions.

## Adaptation

Adaptation is the ability to change course when conditions are different than anticipated. This is a cornerstone of any Agile method, and is unquestionably fostered with Scrum. Work happens in relatively short intervals (one to four weeks) that allow for frequent reviews and feedback from stakeholders and customers. This allows the Scrum team to quickly correct course if needed, before building something too big to pivot.

But adaptation is not only related to the work being done. In fact, Scrum allows for auto-correction of the process itself. If the Scrum team determines that one or more elements of their work process is not satisfactory, it can discuss and review options for improvement. Scrum assumes continuous evolution of processes, work agreements among team members, and supporting systems.

For example, if at some point conditions have changed and the team's "definition of done" is no longer acceptable, they can amend it. Nothing is static. Scrum is considered a framework, as the actual processes and tools used are in continuous evolution.

# HOW SCRUM WORKS

Scrum is an iterative framework composed of a series of events and artifacts. Teams iterate through each cycle following a well-defined schedule of events. At the end of each iteration, the cycle starts all over again. Each cycle is timeboxed and always has the same duration. One cycle of the process is called a Sprint.

## The Sprint

The Sprint, in Scrum, is equivalent to one cycle through the full Scrum process. A Sprint is always timeboxed, i.e. its duration is predefined and always the same. Sprints can last between one and four weeks, and the most common duration is two weeks.

At the beginning of each Sprint, the Product Owner selects a list of items from the Product Backlog based on priority, and presents them to the rest of the team during the Sprint Planning meeting. At the end of this meeting the team produces the Sprint

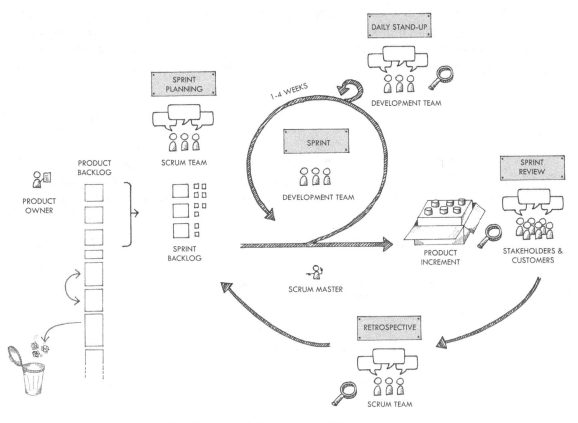

The five events in the Scrum workflow

Backlog, a list of all work the team commits to for the Sprint. The work can then begin.

For the duration of the Sprint the team focuses on delivering the work it has committed to. Every day, it spends a short amount of time (15 minutes) on the Daily Stand-up meeting (also called Daily Scrum). This is an opportunity for each team member to share what they are working on, and any impediments to completing the work.

At the end of the Sprint, the team delivers the Product Increment, the result of the work performed. This is then presented to the stakeholders and customers at the Sprint Review meeting, and they provide validation and feedback to help the team adjust their plan for the next iterations.

As a final step in the Scrum iteration, the team meets for a Retrospective meeting, where the team reviews how it performed the work and uncovers opportunities for improvement. This enables the Scrum process to adapt and self-correct.

The Sprint then ends and the team gets ready to start a new Sprint. Any work that is not completed in the Sprint, or any new work that is created as a result of feedback from the Sprint Review meeting, goes back into the Product Backlog. The Product Owner then reviews all the items and updates the priorities, before a new Sprint can start.

## LEARN MORE

There is so much more to Scrum than what I can include in this book. My goal was to provide a quick overview of Scrum and help you learn its basic principles. If you would like to learn more, there are excellent books and guides on Scrum, including:

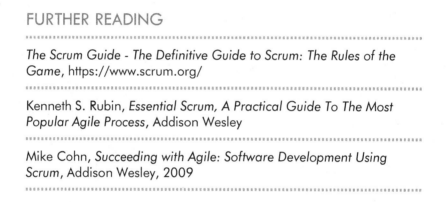

### FURTHER READING

*The Scrum Guide - The Definitive Guide to Scrum: The Rules of the Game*, https://www.scrum.org/

Kenneth S. Rubin, *Essential Scrum, A Practical Guide To The Most Popular Agile Process*, Addison Wesley

Mike Cohn, *Succeeding with Agile: Software Development Using Scrum*, Addison Wesley, 2009

# REFERENCES

1. Wards auto - http://wardsauto.com/datasheet/us-vehicle-sales-market-share-company-1961-2014

2. Various sources including: https://www.forbes.com/sites/bertelschmitt/2016/09/28/worlds-largest-automakers-2016-toyota-pulls-ahead-of-volkswagen-by-a-hair/#2851f5bf1af1

3. Source: Yahoo! Finance, historical data BBRY https://finance.yahoo.com/quote/BBRY/history?period1=1184904000&period2=1256011200&interval=1wk&filter=history&frequency=1wk

4. Source: Gartner 2016 http://www.gartner.com/newsroom/id/3415117

5. Source: Wikipedia "App Store (iOS)" https://en.wikipedia.org/wiki/App_Store_(iOS)

6. Source: Statista "Number of apps available in leading app stores as of June 2016" https://www.statista.com/statistics/276623/number-of-apps-available-in-leading-app-stores/

7. The Agile Manifesto: http://agilemanifesto.org/

8. My former team at Capital One presented this project at Dreamforce 2017 as a success story of developing a new customer platform in retail banking. https://www.salesforce.com/video/1788387/

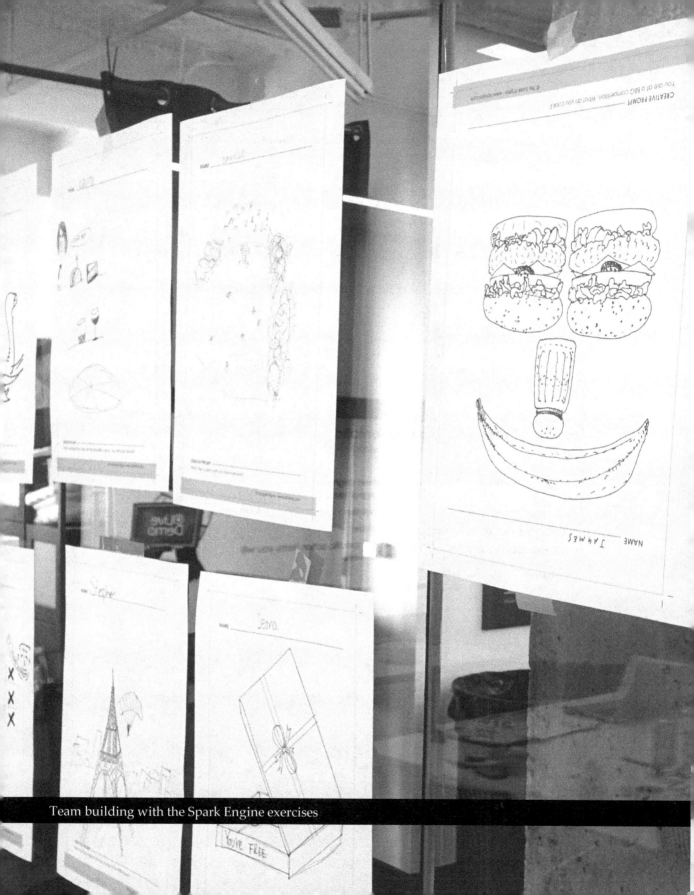

Team building with the Spark Engine exercises

# [5]

# EMPOWER YOUR TEAM

Team empowerment is the process of giving your team the authority to make decisions. When a team is empowered, the decision-making process is no longer top-down, reserved for the manager or the executive running the show. The team participates in the decision-making, proposes ideas and solutions, and takes ownership of tasks and commitments. As a result, when decisions are made collaboratively among team members, broader sets of solutions may be explored, and a stronger sense of commitment is created within the team. When teams feel empowered, their productivity increases, as does the overall quality of the product they are building.

## A CULTURE OF EMPOWERMENT

Empowerment is not to be confused with delegation. Delegation is the act of giving someone else a task to complete and a time frame in which to complete it. With delegation, managers are still expected to supervise and ensure that the task is accomplished with regular check-ins on progress.

Empowerment is about trusting employees to make the right decisions. While delegation is task-based, empowerment is about authority and decision-making.

Your team members know how to do their jobs. They understand their roles, their function within the organization, and their tasks. Often, they have perspectives, experience, and knowledge that allows them to see a better solution than what you alone could see. By letting them take the lead, you build trust in your team, foster a stronger sense of collaboration, and increase commitment in the outcome.

*Your role is to encourage and support the decision-making environment, and to give employees the tools and knowledge they need to make and act upon their own decisions.*[1]

Another trait that goes along with empowerment is the ability to listen. Listening, rather than directing, allows team members to share their ideas, offer alternatives, and collaborate more.

When you give everyone the space and safety to express their opinions and voice their concerns, you will be amazed by the results. Often, the result is a better solution, a stronger commitment by the entire team, and a higher sense of satisfaction among everyone. You may be the ultimate decision-making authority on critical decisions, or help the team unite on a decision together. And that's expected by the leader. The important aspect is that the decision is not imposed top-down, but rather is the result of a healthy, collaborative discussion with the team.

TRY
THIS

## TIPS

Here are some tips to foster an environment of empowerment with your team:

### Empower your product manager

- Give authority to your product manager (or Product Owner, in Scrum) to make decisions on the product — features, backlog, roadmap, priorities, outcomes.

- Make sure the product manager is available to the team, to provide context and answer any questions. Ideally, he or she should be co-located with the team.

- Provide support when needed — access to resources, stakeholders, or customers. Remove impediments. Otherwise let your product manager and your team run the show.

### Empower your development team

- Co-locate your team to foster collaboration and transparency. Remote teams can work effectively, but nothing substitutes for the face-to-face interactions of co-located teams.

- Make sure your development team is cross-functional and allow its members to self-organize their roles and their work.

- Bring the team along when you do customer interviews or exploratory field trips. This helps by building context and making everyone feel more a part of the project. See later in this chapter for a story on exploratory trips.
- Value your engineers and their ideas. They can be great sources of innovation, and can suggest better ways to build a feature to deliver value to your customers.

## Empower your Scrum Master

- The Scrum Master is a change agent and a servant leader to the team. Give him or her the resources and the context he or she needs.
- The Scrum Master is not the secretary of the team. Let the team manage its work and tasks. The Scrum Master should be there to guide the team on how to manage their work and coach them on best practices, not do it for them.

## Empower your leadership

- Build a relationship based on communication, transparency, and respect.
- Share roadmaps, priorities, and backlog. This will let them see the big picture and reduce anxiety about the next MVP.
- Invite the senior leadership to Sprint Reviews and other inspection opportunities. Give them an opportunity to provide feedback on progress and direction on roadmap.
- Leverage your leadership to help you remove impediments.

## Empower your customers

- Bring your customers or end users into the development process by giving visibility to your product increment updates.
- Allow customers to provide feedback often. You may not always do what they ask, but you can always appreciate their input.
- Learn from them, and then validate your insights with prototype testing.

## FURTHER READING

James C. Hunter, *The servant leadership training course* – Audiobook, Audible.com

# TEAM-BUILDING

Team-building is creating a social bond among team members, fostering a sense of trust, and enabling everyone to improve how they work. Every team is different, and may be at a different stage of development. Your team may have already developed its practices or you may bring new methods into your process. In any case, taking care of your team and the well-being of its members is a primary responsibility of leadership.

Here are few ideas to foster team-building:

## Team liftoff

If your team is new, or just started working on a new project, a team liftoff can be a great way to generate context and foster closer connections among team members. Liftoff is an interesting, quick book that provides a multitude of ideas on how to run a liftoff for your team.

### FURTHER READING

"Liftoff: Start and Sustain Successful Agile Teams", 2nd Edition by Diana Larsen, Ainsley Nies

## The spark engine

Over the years, I have found ice breakers to be effective at creating a warmer and safer atmosphere among people, but not at creating long-term connections between them. So, after experimenting with a few different solutions, I have created a series of drawing exercises that team members can do together, and share with each other. They are designed to be small challenges outside the comfort zone, to spark creativity. And because participants share their drawings with each other, the exercise creates a feeling of collaboration, reduces the fear of failure, and develops a memory of other persons.

The drawing part of these exercises is not about quality, or becoming the next Picasso. The act itself is important. Regardless of your skill level and drawing ability, these exercises work for anyone.

Learn more about the book on www.thesparkengine.com

## FURTHER READING

"The Spark Engine: Drawing exercises that ignite team creativity",
Valerio Zanini and others, 5D Vision Publishing, 2nd Edition 2018

## One question a day

This is a simple, yet effective, method to create a culture of sharing and learning among each other in any team. In fact, it's been used in business teams as well as in families. The idea is to ask one question a day, requiring an answer from every team member. Just the process of sharing the answer — as silly as it can be — creates a sense of transparency and lowers the fear of failure among team members.

## FURTHER READING

"Group Glue: The connective power of how simple questions lead to great conversations", Jeffrey T Cook, 2016

## Innovation games

In his book "Innovation Games, Creating Breakthrough Products Through Collaborative Play", Luke Hohmann introduced the idea of games as a way to foster collaboration within teams and generate ideas for successful products.

While you can have fun when playing these games, they have many purposes, including discovering new business opportunities, prioritizing features, collecting feedback, and fostering a culture of collaboration. The book provides a quick reference to each of the games, and an overview of the context in which to use them. It's an easy read, and you can find several ideas to change the way you collaborate with your team on product innovation.

## FURTHER READING

Luke Hohmann, *Innovation Games, creating breakthrough products through collaborative play*, Addison Wesley, 2007

## Design Thinking workshop

I have participated in or facilitated a few Design Thinking workshops for teams at different companies and I find this a great activity to foster a stronger sense of team and learn Design Thinking. The idea is to give the team a challenge (in the form of a problem statement) and then let them go through the Design Thinking motions to solve it. They must collaborate, ideate, build prototypes, and interact with external people (prospective customers). In doing so, they learn how to work with each other and become a closer unit.

## Retrospectives

If you can do only one thing, organize a retrospective with your team. Scrum already prescribes this practice at the end of each Sprint (every 2 weeks, with the usual cadence). Retrospectives are a great way to get feedback and to find ways to improve how you work together with your team.

There are many examples of retrospectives, including the Keep/More/Less, Sailing Boat, and ROTI (Return on Time Invested) exercises — some of my favorites. You can find more on the Tasty Cupcakes website (http://tastycupcakes.org/tag/retrospective/). There are also a few books on the topic.

### FURTHER READING

Tasty Cupcakes: http://tastycupcakes.org/tag/retrospective/

"Agile Retrospectives: Making Good Teams Great", Esther Derby, Diana Larsen, Pragmatic, 2006

## Happy hours

Who doesn't like to get a break from work and spend some time outside the office? Especially when its sunny and warm, or when you have something to celebrate, a happy hour is a great way to share stories with your team, learn more about each other, and why not get a drink at your boss's expense? This is always a fun activity to do, just make sure to organize it responsibly and drive safely :-) (By the way, the happy hour is not about alcohol, it's about spending time together with your team at the end of a busy day, especially outside of the office.)

## Field trips

A field trip is always an opportunity to socialize and learn something new. Take your team out of the office with you on customer interviews, or on exploration trips. This helps building context and making everyone feel more a part of the project.

# EXPLORATION TRIP TO NY

A REAL STORY

When I was at Capital One, working on digital innovation for our bank branches, I took my teams on an exploration trip to New York City every year. Maybe not everybody at the same time, but we always ended up with a large group of participants. Why New York? Because it's such a big city with a multitude of activities taking place. We had customers, so we could visit them and get their feedback on the latest idea or prototype. And we made sure to schedule visits to the coolest innovation stores of the moment. One year it was Time Warner Cable's new flagship store, and then BMW's and Samsung's, and then Apple's. Having exposure to innovation ideas outside of the banking industry allowed my team to stay updated with trends and find better solutions to our problems. There is always something new to learn on a field trip, and it's fun.

There are interesting events and activities happening in every city around the world. Just find the ones that are inspiring for your team's development and creativity, get out of your office, and spend a day or two exploring the world.

# REFERENCES

1. Source: "Empowering Your Employees to Empower Themselves" - Marshall Goldsmith - APRIL 23, 2010 - Harvard Business Review - https://hbr.org/2010/04/empowering-your-employees-to-e

# [PART 3]

## THE FIVE DIMENSIONS

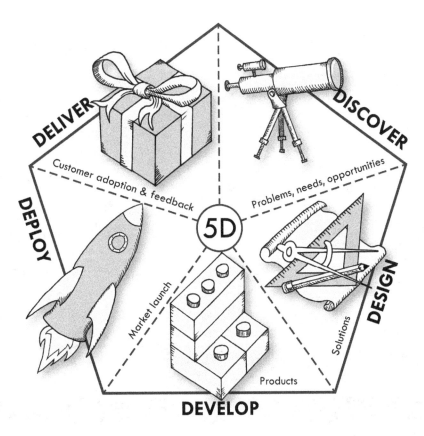

Brainstorming exercise to list activities for human-centered design

# [6]

# THE FIVE DIMENSIONS OF PRODUCT MANAGEMENT

We have become increasingly good at building products. Agile, DevOps, and Lean Startup methodologies have reduced the time to market and the complexity of deploying a new set of features, while improving the quality and shortening the feedback loop with customers. Armed with these methodologies, product managers can ideate, design, and build products in shorter times, and then deploy them in the marketplace.

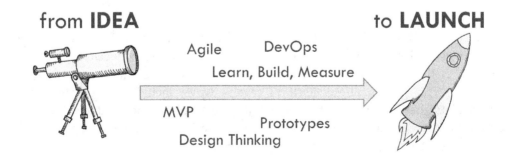

Often, most of the effort is focused on launching the product as soon as possible. However, the goal of building a product should not be launching it in the marketplace. Certainly, we want to have a successful launch, but that should not be the ultimate goal. The goal of building a product should be to deliver value to the end user.

# CLOSING THE DELIVERY GAP

Teams and organizations that focus on launching products rather than delivering value often reflect corporate cultures where the product managers are awarded bonuses or promotions based on products deployed. These companies focus on output. It's the old manufacturing process of getting widgets out of the production line as quickly as possible.

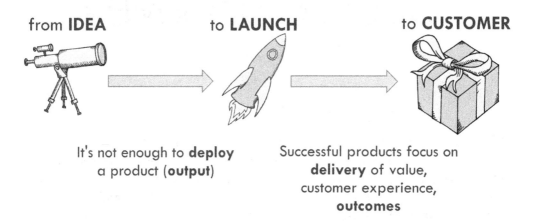

from **IDEA**  to **LAUNCH**  to **CUSTOMER**

It's not enough to **deploy** a product (**output**)

Successful products focus on **delivery** of value, customer experience, **outcomes**

Products should instead be built and launched to deliver outcomes and benefits to the end users. I call this problem the **Delivery Gap**: a gap between deploying a product in the market and delivering value to the end users (and measuring its outcome). This gap manifests itself in several ways, including poorly executed product launches, products that fail to win the marketplace, and products that, once deployed, show a high level of problems that the business then struggles to fix. Companies often struggle to close the gap after the fact.

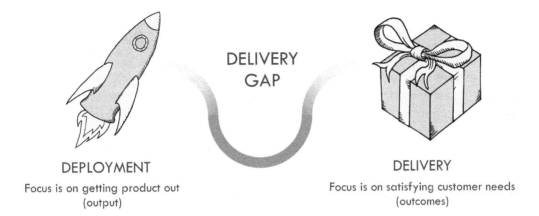

**DELIVERY GAP**

**DEPLOYMENT**
Focus is on getting product out
(output)

**DELIVERY**
Focus is on satisfying customer needs
(outcomes)

To deliver value to the customers and in return generate real value for the business, the organization should focus on delivery, not deployment. It should focus on outcomes (for the customers, for the business), not on output. It should create a culture where cranking out products as quickly as possible is replaced with measuring outcomes and real value delivered to the customer.

The delivery gap was clearly manifested in a product launch by a major bank.[1] After realizing it was a latecomer to the mobile banking revolution, the bank invested a ton of money in developing and finally launching a long-awaited mobile app for its customers. The app allowed them to manage their bank accounts, and included features like depositing checks by taking pictures of them. It was celebrated as a success, and the product manager received a promotion shortly after launching it.

No one thought about measuring performance of the app and evaluating its real benefits. Unknown to the company, the app had a failure rate of 15%, which caused the app to crash 15 times per every 100 uses.

Marketing executed a big push to promote the app, touting it as the latest digital tool to simplify the banking experience of customers. The customers tolerated the error rate and found work-arounds to solve the problems. Because there was no measurement of performance and no feedback loop with customers, nobody had known this. It was discovered accidentally when an employee started expressing concerns about its reliability. At that point, the app had already been in the market for more than a year.

It was a major blow to the reputation of the company and the team had to scramble to fix it. They finally did, and a few months later the company released a much more robust version of the app.

**A REAL STORY**

# EXPANDING SDLC ONTO 5 DIMENSIONS

The Software Development Life Cycle (SDLC) is a process for planning, creating, testing, and deploying a software application or an information system. It is often applied to product development in the digital space. It usually covers a combination of the following phases:

I find that the traditional SDLC model does not properly reflect the complexity of launching a product in today's marketplace and delivering value to your customers. SDLC is represented as a linear set of phases, with little space to incorporate customer focus and adjust the plan along the way. While you may use Agile practices in one or more of these phases, the overall process feels sequential. It does not properly represent today's needs for iterative and adaptive development.

Finally, launching a product in the market does not mean implementing it in production and hoping someone uses it. In today's ultra-competitive world, to launch a successful product you need to have a broader look. You need marketing, training, support, maintenance, retail locations, a sales team, and partnerships with resellers. These may be critical components of your product's customer experience and should be planned and integrated within your product development activities, not left out as afterthoughts. We need to expand the traditional view of SDLC with a broader framework.

Companies cannot afford to manage projects as a sequential list of phases. Product development should be managed as a cross-dimensional project to break the silos between each phase and reduce the risk of dependencies. Projects should not only be cross-dimensional, but also employ cross-functional teams to break their organizational silos. Product managers cannot work on one dimension at a time, move on to the next one when ready, and hope that everything flows nicely. They should employ a 5-Dimensional vision of their product. This requires looking at a product from the 5 Dimensions of:

Discover, Design, Develop, Deploy, Deliver

Having a 5D vision does not mean that you should work at each phase at the same time. It means that you should think about your Deploy & Deliver plan as early as possible, ideally during Design, so that you have time to put into motion all the different pieces you need, and avoid launching a new product without a fully prepared plan for commercialization.

Having a 5D vision across the entire product development cycle allows you to be agile across the entire process and not just in individual phases.

The 5 Dimensions framework enables organizations to broaden their focus to the entire product development life cycle, from ideation to delivery. It provides support and focus on the Delivery phase, and helps companies measure outcomes and close the delivery gap.

# THE 5D VISION OF GREAT PRODUCTS

To properly understand customer needs, build a solution, and deliver a customer experience that satisfies those needs, product managers need to have a full vision of their product. This is what I call the "5D vision of great products".

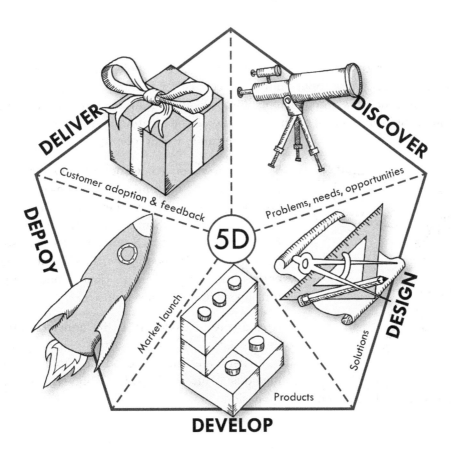

Much like you see an object in the real world from a variety of different angles, the product's 5D vision allows you to view a product across a variety of dimensions as it moves from ideation to launch. Each dimension covers a specific stage in the product development process and includes the elements needed to create a product and deliver a great customer experience. Only by covering all five dimensions can product managers plan and launch successful products in the marketplace.

Product managers need to consider, plan, and execute in all 5 Dimensions to create great products. None of these dimensions is isolated from each other, and they may not even happen in linear order. In fact, you may return to any dimension at any time, and continue iterating through them, as you move forward in your ideation and development activities.

Throughout the book, we refer to these 5 Dimensions of the product vision as we discuss different tools and techniques product managers can use at different phases. Each phase focuses on one dimension at a time and employs a specific set of methodologies. The 5 Dimensions Canvas at the end of this chapter provides a quick look at the different tools and methodologies you can use to cover each dimension.

## DISCOVER

The **Discover** dimension focuses on understanding the problem and customer needs, or identifying an unmet opportunity. Much like an explorer of old, the product manager uses the tools available to explore new areas, learn the terrain, and identify new opportunities. The goal of this exploration is the identification of a clear problem and opportunity worth solving.

The Discovery of a new opportunity may come from a variety of sources including technology advancements (e.g. R&D in new battery technology at Tesla), a market change (e.g. financial incentives for Solar installations), a human need (e.g. social networking in Facebook), or the re-invention of an entire industry (e.g. Uber and Lyft's transformation of the taxi industry).

At the core of Discovery is the understanding of the needs, aspirations, and challenges of customers, and this places ethnographic research methods like Empathy Interviews and Observations at the center of this dimension.

## DESIGN

The **Design** dimension is dedicated to identifying a solution to the problem or need discovered in the previous phase. The goal is to validate an idea for problem/solution fit. Often, there is not a single, clearly defined solution, but rather there are multiple possible solutions. Prototype Testing and Design Thinking help you ideate solutions, narrow the possibilities, and validate your ideas using prototypes and user feedback.

## DEVELOP

The **Development** dimension is when you work with your technology team to create your new product or feature. This is when the hard work put into the Discovery and Design phases come to life, in the form of an actual product that your users can interact with.

The key activity here is to minimize risk and the cost of change by building the product in iterations and enabling your end users to inspect and provide feedback. Plans may adapt along the way, and you may pivot to Discover or Design a new idea if necessary. This kind of agility in development reduces the cost of change, and creates the foundation for a more successful end product.

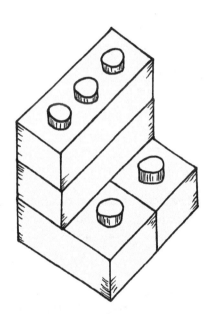

To help the team develop the right product and in the right way, at this stage you should focus on prioritization and keep your technical debt in check. If your goal is to launch a Minimum Viable Product (MVP) in the shortest time and with the fewest resources as possible, work with your cross-functional team and identify the key elements of your overall customer experience, including what you need in Deploy and Deliver. Focus on these elements, and delay everything else.

## DEPLOY

Launching a product in market is probably the most exciting time for a product team. Deployment is a carefully orchestrated set of activities that happen in a particular

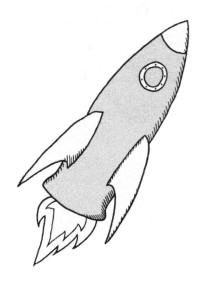

order and that involve multiple teams. Deployment is not only the job of IT Operations, but is a cross-functional team effort. Team members from Marketing, Training, Customer Support, Sales, and other departments come together to orchestrate a successful launch of the new product.

By focusing early on the **Deploy** dimension you can identify what you need for a successful launch across your multi-disciplinary team. You can start planning in the Design and Development phases, and in Deploy everything comes together as the cross-functional team works as a unit for a successful launch.

## DELIVER

The goal of a new product is to bring to life the initial promise set up by the product's vision and satisfy customer needs and expectations. Just having a product in market does not represent success. Only when you can measure and validate the

customer experience your product delivers, can you can measure success. The goal of this phase is to validate your market-solution fit through measurement and customer feedback.

Because **Delivery** is the end goal of product development, the activities in this phase cannot be an afterthought. Proper planning in earlier phases for how you are going to measure and validate your product's success is key to deliver a great product that customers love.

# THE RISK OF A LINEAR APPROACH TO PRODUCT DEVELOPMENT

Even as you approach your work across all 5 Dimensions, the temptation is to cover one phase at a time, and move through them sequentially. You may do the full Discovery, then the full Design, and so on. This linear approach is represented in the figure below.

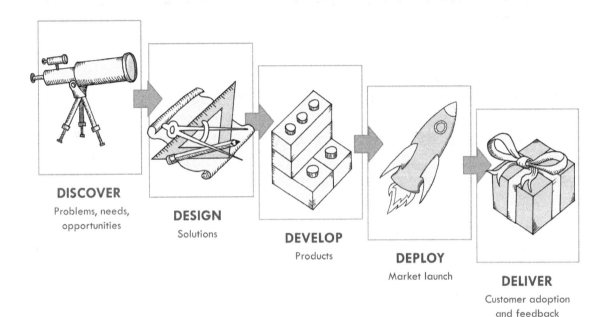

**DISCOVER**
Problems, needs, opportunities

**DESIGN**
Solutions

**DEVELOP**
Products

**DEPLOY**
Market launch

**DELIVER**
Customer adoption and feedback

Notice that some phases may take longer than others. For example, traditionally, a lot of time is spent in Development, while very little is spent in Delivery. This reflects the traditional approach based on SDLC that is focused on building a product, not on delivering a customer experience around that product.

Another problem that stems from approaching the process sequentially is that the risk of change increases exponentially. As you move through each of the phases and as you get closer to Delivery, if changes to the plan are needed, the cost of those changes increase. The cost is higher the more you need to go back to make the change.

Having a 5D vision across the entire product development cycle allows you to be agile across the entire process, and not just in individual phases.

## THE 5D ITERATIVE AND ADAPTIVE APPROACH

Instead of completing all the work in one phase and then moving to the next, consider splitting the work in small increments. Each increment has a view across the 5 Dimensions, from Discovery through Delivery. The idea here is that as you begin Discovery of a new product idea and Design of a solution, you can start integrating how you will launch the solution in Deploy and how you will measure success in Delivery. All this before you even start Development on your idea. This approach gives you a perspective on all the different pieces your cross-functional team needs to work on.

MVP

V.2.0

V.3.0

By slicing your work into smaller increments, you reduce the risk of change. Because you have only worked at a small piece of your overall idea, if you find a problem after you launch and need to make a change, the cost of that change will be small compared to the one you would have had to cover if you had built the whole thing at once.

This approach also helps in thinking about your MVP. The Minimum Viable Product should be conceived across all 5 Dimensions so that you can validate the full customer experience with your product and not just some functionalities. By slicing your work into increments and focusing on all 5 Dimensions for each increment, you deliver a product that your customers can use, and you get validated feedback on the overall product delivery plan and customer experience. This reduces your risk of failure, decreases the cost of change, and increases the chances that your customers love the product you build.

# THE 5D VISION CANVAS

There are many tools and methodologies product managers and their teams can use at each phase in product development. The following canvas provides an at-a-glance view of the 5 Dimensions and the tools and methodologies to employ for each.

The following chapters provide an explanation of the most important tools for each phase, and useful tips to implement them in your daily job.

The 5D Vision Canvas is also available for download at:

https://www.5dvision.com/docs/5d-canvas/

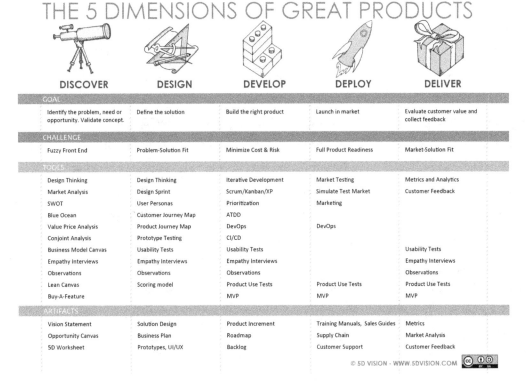

## THE 5 DIMENSIONS OF GREAT PRODUCTS

| | DISCOVER | DESIGN | DEVELOP | DEPLOY | DELIVER |
|---|---|---|---|---|---|
| **GOAL** | Identify the problem, need or opportunity. Validate concept. | Define the solution | Build the right product | Launch in market | Evaluate customer value and collect feedback |
| **CHALLENGE** | Fuzzy Front End | Problem-Solution Fit | Minimize Cost & Risk | Full Product Readiness | Market-Solution Fit |
| **TOOLS** | Design Thinking | Design Thinking | Iterative Development | Market Testing | Metrics and Analytics |
| | Market Analysis | Design Sprint | Scrum/Kanban/XP | Simulate Test Market | Customer Feedback |
| | SWOT | User Personas | Prioritization | Marketing | |
| | Blue Ocean | Customer Journey Map | ATDD | | |
| | Value Price Analysis | Product Journey Map | DevOps | DevOps | |
| | Conjoint Analysis | Prototype Testing | CI/CD | | |
| | Business Model Canvas | Usability Tests | Usability Tests | | Usability Tests |
| | Empathy Interviews | Empathy Interviews | Empathy Interviews | | Empathy Interviews |
| | Observations | Observations | Observations | | Observations |
| | Lean Canvas | Scoring model | Product Use Tests | Product Use Tests | Product Use Tests |
| | Buy-A-Feature | | MVP | MVP | MVP |
| **ARTIFACTS** | Vision Statement | Solution Design | Product Increment | Training Manuals, Sales Guides | Metrics |
| | Opportunity Canvas | Business Plan | Roadmap | Supply Chain | Market Analysis |
| | 5D Worksheet | Prototypes, UI/UX | Backlog | Customer Support | Customer Feedback |

© 5D VISION - WWW.5DVISION.COM

# THE 5 DIMENSIONS OF GREAT PRODUCTS

  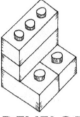

| DISCOVER | DESIGN | DEVELOP |
|---|---|---|
| **GOAL** | | |
| Identify the problem, need or opportunity. Validate concept. | Define the solution | Build the right product |
| **CHALLENGE** | | |
| Fuzzy Front End | Problem-Solution Fit | Minimize Cost & Risk |
| **TOOLS** | | |
| Design Thinking | Design Thinking | Iterative Development |
| Market Analysis | Design Sprint | Scrum/Kanban/XP |
| SWOT | User Personas | Prioritization |
| Blue Ocean | Customer Journey Map | ATDD |
| Value Price Analysis | Product Journey Map | DevOps |
| Conjoint Analysis | Prototype Testing | CI/CD |
| Business Model Canvas | Usability Tests | Usability Tests |
| Empathy Interviews | Empathy Interviews | Empathy Interviews |
| Observations | Observations | Observations |
| Lean Canvas | Scoring model | Product Use Tests |
| Buy-A-Feature | | MVP |
| **ARTIFACTS** | | |
| Vision Statement | Solution Design | Product Increment |
| Opportunity Canvas | Business Plan | Roadmap |
| 5D Worksheet | Prototypes, UI/UX | Backlog |

| DEPLOY | DELIVER |
| --- | --- |
| Launch in market | Evaluate customer value and collect feedback |
| Full Product Readiness | Market-Solution Fit |
| Market Testing | Metrics and Analytics |
| Simulate Test Market | Customer Feedback |
| Marketing | |
| DevOps | |
| | Usability Tests |
| | Empathy Interviews |
| | Observations |
| Product Use Tests | Product Use Tests |
| MVP | MVP |
| Training Manuals, Sales Guides | Metrics |
| Supply Chain | Market Analysis |
| Customer Support | Customer Feedback |

# REFERENCES

1. This story is the result of several interviews with key members of the project, and personal experience as a customer

# NOTES

A Customer Journey Map is a great tool to discover opportunities in the customer experience

# [7]

# DISCOVER

The act of discovery is the intentional, or sometimes unexpected, search for a customer problem, a business opportunity, or an unsolved need in the marketplace. The goal of the Discover phase is to identify a need or an opportunity, and then validate that it is a clear pain point for customers, a transformational change, or a lucrative opportunity in the market. An idea for a new product can come from a variety of sources: market trends and new business opportunities; technological breakthroughs; customer insights or unmet needs; market adjacencies. Any source of insight is worth exploring and may open opportunities for a new product.

Sometimes a new idea comes from a technology breakthrough: e.g. Gore-Tex was born from the casual discovery of expansion properties of the PTFE polymer and since the Dupont leadership was not interested in its market applications, W. L. Gore started his own company. Ideas can come from an untapped opportunity: Apple had a first-mover advantage in the purchase of a new miniaturized hard-drive that could make the iPod store much more music than its competitors, but its ultimate success was in solving the need for an integrated and easy-to-use method to buy and store music which was introduced with iTunes.

At times, new product ideas are not generated from a specific customer problem, a market need or a technological breakthrough, but through a combination of factors that bring to life a new vision, a "blue ocean strategy".[1] This often leads to the reinvention of entire new markets, much like Uber has done with the transportation market and Amazon has done with the book distribution market.

Breakthrough innovations don't happen every day. And even if you have an idea that can revolutionize the world, you may still want to properly assess your idea and validate customer needs before investing in its development. At this stage, you should be focused on understanding the problem, not yet on building the solution. The challenge is that the problem, its underlying drivers and customer needs, may not yet be clearly defined. The lack of well-defined data complicates the evaluation, and that is why this phase is often called the "fuzzy front end" of product development.[2]

Validating your ideas with customers before moving on to the development of a solution reduces the risks of working on the wrong idea, or possibly solving the wrong problem. It also offers the opportunity to understand who your real customers (or customer segments) may be, and to define in more clarity your market strategy for launching the new product.

If asked directly, customers may not be able to grasp the potential benefits of a new product, because truly innovative concepts may require too much of an imaginative leap for them to grasp. Sometimes, an opportunity is just too innovative for the times, but when customers finally try it they may fall in love with it (e.g. when the Apple iPhone first came out, asked for a comparison with the Blackberry phone, people preferred the physical keyboard of the Blackberry to the touchscreen keyboard of the iPhone. Yet, a year later, the Blackberry phone was history and physical keyboards on phones have now almost disappeared).

The key activities in this stage are research and learning. Invest time with your customers, understand their needs, and validate a possible business opportunity. Do the same with your technology and business teams. Create alignment around a common idea, need, and vision.

Time spent in discovery and in understanding customer needs is time well-spent. Regarding the importance of defining the problem, Albert Einstein said, "If I had an hour to solve a problem, I'd spend 55 minutes thinking about the problem and five minutes thinking about solutions."

# OBSERVING CUSTOMERS IN THEIR CONTEXT

Observing your customers in their own context is one of the most powerful learning opportunities at your disposal. It allows you to dive into the customer's reality, see things how they see them, and understand what compels them to take certain actions.

We often create mental images and hypotheses of our customers and of their behaviors, and only by observing them in their real context can we validate or (often) change our initial assumptions. Observations help to validate your hypotheses, or to learn something new about a customer need or their use of your product.

## In person

You can learn a lot by observing your target users as they go about their business in their real environments. Notice not only what they do, but also how they do it. Pair with an interview to discover the why behind their actions.

## In a simulated environment

Recreate the environment you'd like to study and observe people behind a one-way mirror, record their actions for later review, or use eye-tracking technologies to investigate usability issues.

## Online and remote

If you don't have direct access to customers, there are many tools that allow tracking user behavior online and collecting statistics of what they do and what they use more frequently on your website or app.

Observations and interviews can easily go together to collect direct feedback from customers, however they explore different domains and can provide different insights. Observations may not help answer the "why" question (interviews can), but can provide visibility into "what" customers do with your product and "how" they do it, in ways that they may not be able to describe with words.

Performing observations is not easy. It's not just a matter of being very attentive to details. Doing observations right is like the difference between watching a game and being there with the players. Even if you have a good seat and feel the sweat of the game, you are still observing the players with a remote lens. If you were able to run on the field, pass the ball, sweat it yourself, then you would really know what it is like to play the game: what split-second decisions players need to make, what sudden changes of course they take, and how it feels to know where the other teammates are at any given moment.

The point here is that observations require a shift of perspective: you need to immerse yourself in the customer's context. And you can only learn if you change your perspective to that of the customer. Figuratively, you need to walk in your customer's shoes to really know how it feels to be a customer. Only then you can discover the inner needs, pain points, and aspirations of your customers.

A REAL
STORY

# LIVING RICH VERSUS BEING RICH

When we research customers, we tend to bring our biases and interpret what we see with the lenses of our beliefs. It's hard to let go of assumptions and previous knowledge and really shift perspectives to see the reality of people. An example of this bias is the fascination that most of us share for rich and wealthy people. We imagine the lives of these customers — they probably live in vast estates with four-car garages, drive Ferraris, own yachts and private planes, shop at Tiffany's, and wear Ferragamo shoes. In other words, we imagine the rich and wealthy like Leonardo Di Caprio in "The Wolf of Wall Street".

There are certainly many people who can afford this glamorous lifestyle. However, when you look across the broader population for wealthy individuals (defined as those having a personal net worth of at least $1 million) the story can be very different. Reality is much closer to the picture described in the book "The Millionaire Next Door: The Surprising Secrets of America's Wealthy".[3]

The authors spent years researching the rich and wealthy in America, visiting these people at their homes and observing how they go about their daily lives. What they found explains what we normally don't see beneath the tip of the iceberg and is fascinating because it goes against the common bias we have. Typically, high net-worth individuals have accumulated their wealth over the course of their lifetimes by saving more than the average American. The wealthy have no Ferrari and do not drink Veuve Clicquot from crystal flutes served on silver trays. They do not spend indiscriminately or live extravagantly. Instead, they save their pennies, live frugal lives, and value financial stability.

If you are building a product aimed at wealthy individuals (e.g. a French-inspired new premium wine, or a customized financial investment product), knowing what your customers value and how they prioritize their expenses could be an important insight.

FURTHER READING

Thomas J. Stanley and William D. Danko, *The Millionaire Next Door: The Surprising Secrets of America's Wealthy*, Taylor Trade Publishing, 2010

# EMPATHY INTERVIEWS

Through empathy interviews we are still seeking to learn about customer needs, wants, and expectations, but we do this by engaging even more directly with the customer and asking them specifically about their needs, wants, frustrations, and motivations. They are a core constituent of human-centered design as they allow your research team to shift perspective and connect with your customers at an emotional level.

*Empathy: the ability to understand and share the feelings of another*

- Google dictionary

Empathy interviews complement a broad set of exploration techniques that include observations, prototype testing, and customer journey maps. The goal of empathy interviews is to uncover the deeper motivations that drive customer needs and choices. They help you understand not only what customers do and how they do it, but also, and more importantly, why they do it. Answering the "why?" allows you to identify deeper needs and discover insights that guide the design of your solutions.

Empathy interviews can be used at any stage in the product development. During Discover, they are a powerful tool to uncover needs and opportunities for new potential products. During Design and Develop, they help to validate that you are building the right product. And during the later stages of Deploy and Deliver, they help uncover additional areas of opportunity and validate whether you have met the customer expectations.

The key is frequency: the more often you seek customer feedback during your development cycle, the more likely you are to build something that customers really value.

# GOOZEX SHIPPING LABELS

I was first introduced to the concept of empathy interviews when I was leading Goozex.com — the largest online video game trading platform.[4,5] My team and I met regularly with a group of customers to exchange ideas and get their feedback. We did this in person, through quarterly events with the local community of users, and online using our discussion forum.

One day we met with a gentleman and his son — I will call them Adam and Billy. Adam was in his late thirties and his son Billy was in elementary school (roughly third or fourth grade). The son, Billy, was a video gamer and an avid user of our trading system. So much so that he ran a little side business in his class.

His school friends were also video gamers, but unlike Billy, they didn't have a computer, or easy access to a Goozex account. So, Billy offered to do video game transactions on their behalf. He collected the used video games they wanted to get rid of, and traded them on Goozex. When he received another video game in return, he brought it to his friends at school — keeping tabs of who owned what. Each transaction cost Billy about $3.50 (between fees and shipping), and he charged his friends $5 — making a $1.50 profit from each trade.

Adam was proud of his son and of his entrepreneurial activities. However, he confessed to us that this came with a pain point. Because every video game had to be shipped, his son would package the video games during the week, and then the two of them would make a trip to the post office every Saturday. While the trip to the post office was a bonding time between father and son, Adam confessed that it was also quite a pain, given the long lines. He wished there were a better way to ship the packages while avoiding the lines at the post office.

We did some more research with other customers and learned that, like Adam, people loved the service provided by Goozex, but they hated going to the post office to ship their games. We also identified other pain points related to shipping. For example, they often placed stamps on the package at home before going to the post office. But since they didn't know the right shipping rate, they ended up overpaying or underpaying with the risk that the game would be returned to them by the post office for insufficient postage.

These insights sparked the development of a new service that we called, without much creativity, "shipping labels". We gave our users the ability to pay for and print a shipping label directly off their computer. They could then just drop the package in a mailbox to ship it. Using exact weight information for every video game, we were able to calculate the exact shipping rate the customer had to pay, and avoid issues of over/under-payment. In short, customers didn't have to go to the post office anymore, and they could manage their Goozex transactions from the comfort of their home.

At the time, this was a breakthrough innovation as no other competitor offered this service. Even the US postal service did not allow purchasing of shipping labels from its website. We integrated with a USPS partner to give us the shipping rates and generate the barcodes, and with Amazon, Walmart, and a few other online retailers to collect the exact weight information of each product.

Because we added a $0.50 convenience fee for each shipping label, we also generated a new revenue stream. Customers were happy to pay the additional fee to avoid a trip to the post office.

In the end, Adam let us know that he loved the new feature and he was thankful to have his Saturday mornings back. His son Billy's school business was thriving and he could now ship his games any day of the week from home.

## STRUCTURE OF AN EMPATHY INTERVIEW

### Prepare the interview

The day before the interview, meet with your team and discuss the objectives you'd like to achieve. This creates alignment and ensures that everyone is on-board with the research. Write down a list of assumptions you have going into the interviews, and core hypotheses you would like to validate during the interviews. This can be a short list, but it's important to be mindful of your own assumptions and hypotheses as you explore your product idea with real people.

Next, prepare a list of high-level questions. Interviews should not be scripted — they should be a relatively free-flowing conversation. But a list of high-level questions helps keep the team focused on the overall objectives and provides a level of comfort during the interview process.

Prepare any supporting materials you may need. These may include worksheets to guide the interview and take notes, prototypes to share with customers and get feedback on, and recording tools such as cameras or audio recorder apps on your phone.

## Team structure

You need two to three people: One interviewer, one or two note-takers

The interviewer is the one asking questions, the note-taker(s) jot(s) down answers, observations, and key insights. The team can switch roles after each interview to give everyone a chance to practice, and possibly avoid any bias a single interviewer may have. This is not required, but more a matter of preference.

During the interview, focus on what you hear (answers to your questions), what you see (body language, non-verbal cues), and what your customer is doing and feeling (emotions, beliefs, frustrations).

Use the templates for empathy interviews provided in this book to support the discovery and note-taking of insights.

## Running an empathy interview

I normally schedule interviews using one-hour slots. I then divide the interview into three sections.

- Interview: 25-45 minutes

- Debrief within the team: 10-15 minutes

- Break between interviews: 5 minutes

Depending on the specific learning you are trying to achieve, you can use a shorter format or adjust the schedule as needed.

### Interview: 25-45 minutes

This is roughly divided in three parts:

*Introduction*

Start with introducing yourself (your name, who you are, the company you work for if needed) and the purpose of the project. Why are you are doing this research, and what you hope to learn from it.

Then ask your interviewee to introduce themselves. Without getting too personal, you may ask how they feel today or how they feel about this interview. This initial introduction is very useful as it helps the interviewee become comfortable with the situation, and the two of you to establish rapport.

*Interview*

This is the main interview time that you use to learn about the person's needs, pain points, and aspirations. Remember that the purpose of this interview is not to go robotically through a list of questions and record the answers. The purpose is to connect at an emotional level and learn about the motivations, aspirations, and expectations of your customers. Often, it's not what they say, but rather how they say it that matters. Observe the body language and the facial expressions. Try to pick up on emotions or signs of discomfort.

To ensure that you establish an emotional bond with your interviewee, be an active listener and follow up on key points or comments they make. Often, asking a follow up question shows that you are listening. Go off-script. Follow the flow.

*Wrap-up*

This is the time used to wrap up the interview. Thank your interviewee for their time and express appreciation for what you have learned.

Then, offer the opportunity to share anything more they'd like to share. When you wrap things up and say thank you, the interviewee's emotional state relaxes as they feel they have done their part. As they relax, new thoughts may come to mind, and they may be able to share some new insights, or open up on a different level. Be prepared to seize this opportunity for learning if it presents itself.

## Debrief within the team: 10-15 minutes

After you have finished the interview, find a quiet place with your team and review the findings of the last interview. Share key insights or memorable moments, and jot them down. You can do this after each interview so that memories are fresh, or at the end of the day. The goal is to share what you learned and develop a common understanding of the problems or needs identified.

I find it useful to jot things down on Post-It notes as this makes it easier for synthesis later, but writing on a notepad is equally effective. Choose what works best for you.

## Break between interviews: 5 minutes

Give yourself some slack as you will need a break after the first few interviews. Having a little break allows your brain to regain energy between interviews.

## Tips to conduct interviews

### Conduct interviews in person

With today's technology, we can perform remote interviews using Skype, Whatsapp, and other applications. While this is possible, completing them in person is always the preferred format. Not only do you get a better sense of your interviewee's body language and other visual cues, but you may also be able to observe the customer in their context.

### Ask "Why?" questions

"Why?" is probably the most important question you should ask. Ask it as often as you can without sounding as if you are questioning the customer's judgment. Often, it's not what a customer says, does, or feels that matters, but why they do what they do that is important. The why question is the one that usually leads to real insights.

### Ask open-ended questions

Always use open-ended questions. The goal is to learn about your customer and explore as much as possible. You don't want to restrain your learning opportunities by asking narrow questions.

Instead of asking "Would you prefer it in blue or red?", ask instead "What color would you prefer?" Open-ended questions lead to a broader variety of answers.

### Silence is powerful

Use silence to your advantage. When the interviewee has completed their answer and you feel you'd like to learn more, wait a few seconds. Often, they'll feel the pressure to fill the silence and will tell you more.

## Sketch a solution

At times, ask your customers to take a blank piece of paper and draw their ideal solution. This often leads to interesting insights as they may not be able to express in words what they can draw. Not everyone is a gifted artist, but they don't need to be. You are not looking for the next Picasso, but rather are looking for a sketch that triggers ideas.

## Take a photo

With their permission, take a photo of the interviewee. Save this photo along with the notes you have taken. This will help you remember the person behind those notes which reminds you of the human needs that are driving your product. Depending on the situation (or your Legal department's advice) you may need to obtain a signed release for photos/video recordings.

## Bring a prototype

If you are at a stage where you have a rough idea of your solution, show a prototype and ask for feedback. The prototype can be anything from a sketch on a napkin to a hi-res app running on your phone. The goal is to validate with your customer whether you are on the right track, and learn if there are any changes you need to make. If you decide to show a prototype, it's better to wait until the second half of the interview to do so because a prototype can focus the interview too narrowly on your idea, rather than encouraging open exploration.

## Bring your development team along

Development teams build the products but rarely interact with their end users. Empathy interviews and observations are great opportunities to provide your development team direct exposure to the customers and their context. This is a powerful experience for your team members because they can more deeply understand the human needs they are working to solve, and it creates a deeper bond within the team.

## NUMBER OF INTERVIEWS

The number of interviews you need to do depends on what you are looking for. For feedback on a specific feature, you may need just a handful. For broad exploration across a variety of segments or geographic areas, you may need more.

There are many studies on how many interviews you need for a full discovery. One of these studies recommends 30 interviews, each lasting about 45 minutes, to source close to 100% of customer needs. With 20 interviews, you get about 90% of needs.[6]

Generally, five to seven interviews are a good start. These will usually yield enough inputs and provide some key insights. You can conduct this number of interviews in a day and get an idea of the direction you need to go.

## FINDING CUSTOMERS

The term "customers" for observations or empathy interviews can apply to a variety of people, depending on the type of product, industry, or learning objective, and in general identifies with the people using your product or service (also called "end users").

### Existing customers

If your sales team allows it, you can reach out to existing customers. Your company has a database of customers — you just need to pull up a list of those living in your area and filter them based on your needs.

If you provide your service at a physical location (rather than online), then you simply need to schedule a visit at that location and find your customers there. Usually, you'll have to get some sort of permission from Legal or Operations.

### Non-customers

Sometimes reaching out to customers is not an easy task, for example, if you are running an online business where they may be spread around the country or even around the world. In these situations, if you cannot find your actual customers, you can use proxies — people in your community that share the same needs, demographics, or aspirations of your customers or potential customers.

## Proxy users

Inside your organization, you may have employees who are very knowledgeable about your customers' needs because they interact with the customers directly (for example your sales people or contact centers). These employees can serve as proxy customers. Using proxies is not an ideal solution because they are still one step removed from the customers, but sometimes they are the best option available.

## Extreme users

To help discover unusual needs and learn of off-the-beaten-path use cases for your product, it is sometimes useful to connect with "extreme users". These are people who have amplified needs and stronger points of view, and may offer insights into highly technical or niche issues.

For example, if you are redesigning the economy seating on a passenger plane, you may want to look for extreme users who are frequent flyers, who fly with infant children, or who are unable to sleep in-flight. The experiences these users can share may be more insightful than what you may learn from your average passenger with no special needs.

# INTERVIEWING PEOPLE OUTSIDE OF OUR CUSTOMER POOL

A REAL STORY

For one of the projects I did at Capital One, we wanted to learn why customers visited our bank locations and what needs pushed them to drive (often several miles) to a branch rather than going online or calling a hotline. We organized an empathy interview session with six interviewees. Only one of them happened to be a Capital One customer. For our research, we determined that it didn't matter if someone was our customer or was banking at some other institution. What mattered was their need to visit a bank branch. So we searched for and interviewed a group of people who were customers of any bank. What we learned applied very well to the regular Capital One customers too.

# CAPITAL ONE INTERNAL CONSULTANTS AS PROXIES

A REAL STORY

At Capital One we had a team of consultants who traveled around to every bank location and provided support to our bankers. My team designed digital tools for our bankers, and from time to time we needed to get feedback from them on our work. When getting in front of a banker was not possible (due to scheduling conflicts, limited branch hours, inability to travel), we invited the consultants to our office. They lived day-by-day next to our bankers, and knew their challenges and aspirations. The consultants proved to be excellent proxies for our bankers, at least in the early stages of exploration.

## HOW TO RECRUIT PEOPLE TO INTERVIEW

There are many ways to find people to conduct customer research, and your organization may already have an established process to identify them. Here are a few useful tips:

### Craigslist or other bulletin boards

Craigslist can be an easy way to find people interested in your research. To make sure you find people in your target segment, state what you are looking for in your ad, or schedule a brief screening call with each candidate to quickly validate if they satisfy your requirements for the interview. The day of the interview, invite them to your office, or local coffee shop or hotel lobby. Offer them a small token of appreciation for their time, for example, a Starbucks or Amazon gift card.

### Getting help from recruiting companies

There are companies that specialize in finding candidates for interviews, focus groups, and research in general. These companies can be an excellent source of users for your research as they can also help in crafting a user profile. They will filter the people for you, and will send you the number of people you need.

Some of these companies will do the research for you. While convenient, I don't like this approach because it creates an intermediary between me and the people I'm trying to connect with, and the end results may be inadvertently filtered by the company's researchers.

## Reaching out to existing customers

Existing customers offer the advantage that you already have data on them. This makes it easier to filter your users and find those that may be more interesting for your research. Even if your business is only online and you have never met them, there may be customers who are more than willing to come meet with you in person to help improve a product they like.

## Intercepting people

You may go to a local coffee shop or a shopping mall and intercept random people there. If you approach them kindly and explain what you are trying to do, many people are willing to spend a few minutes to offer their thoughts on your ideas. The problem with intercepts is that people are not screened, so they may not represent your target segment. But intercepts can be useful when you are looking for a broad set of feedbacks or are investigating a problem that is common.

## TEMPLATES FOR INTERVIEWS

The following pages offer a few templates that you can use to guide your interviews and to collect feedback from your users. Feel free to copy them and carry with you at your interviews. You may need multiple copies of each template, at least one per interviewee.

### DOWNLOAD

https://www.5dvision.com/docs/empathy-interviews-dt/

EMPATHY INTERVIEW WORKSHEET
# USER DEBRIEF

**HOW TO USE THIS**

Prepare a sheet for each person you interview, and summarize what you learn during the interview in the boxes below.

User's photo or drawing

**NAME**

**OCCUPATION / ROLE**

**OTHER NOTES**

**MOST PRESSING NEEDS**
What are this user's most pressing needs?

**MAIN INSIGHTS**
What key insights did you learn today?

**PROBLEM SOLVING**
What other ways could you help solve the problem?

EMPATHY INTERVIEW WORKSHEET

# OBSERVATIONS

**USERS**
Who are the users?

**ACTIVITIES**
What are they doing?

**INTERACTIONS**
What interactions you see between people, tools, and space?

**QUOTES AND INSIGHTS**
What are key quotes you hear? Key insights you gather?

EMPATHY INTERVIEW WORKSHEET

# EMOTIONAL JOURNEY MAP

**HOW TO USE THIS**

Ask your user to tell you a story. Jot down their emotional journey throughout the story. What made them happy? What made them sad?

**POSITIVE FEELINGS**

Time

**NEGATIVE FEELINGS**

EMPATHY INTERVIEW WORKSHEET
# INTENT DEEP DIVE

**INTENT**
What are they trying to do?

**ACTIVITY**
How are they doing it?

**MOTIVATION**
Why are they doing it?

# UNDERSTAND YOUR MARKET AND OPPORTUNITY

No product can succeed without proper knowledge and understanding of the market it is living in. A key responsibility of product managers is to maximize the Return-on-Investment (ROI) of their product. Hence, an understanding of the market, competition, opportunity, and customer segments is essential to properly plan your product.

In general, market analysis can be performed in a multitude of ways, looking at industry trends, competitors, internal and external factors (e.g. new regulation), technology breakthroughs that may revolutionize a market (e.g. Apple was the first company to take advantage of a new 2.5" compact hard-drive, and leapfrog its competitors with the first iPod), and customer segmentation.

Often, an understanding of market dynamics brings to life new opportunities. Think about the advent of private space companies (SpaceX and others). The technology to build and launch missiles has been around for dozens of years, but the market created the opportunity for these private companies to flourish only in recent years, after NASA canceled the Space Shuttle program and restructured its financial planning to allow for external suppliers to compete for its business.

If you are new to a market, a useful way to begin your discovery is to immerse yourself in the lives of your customers. Leave your office and go on an exploration tour. Meet with customers (and partners, suppliers, distributors) and learn as much as possible about their needs, hopes, and pain points — we discussed Observations and Empathy Interviews earlier in this chapter. Then meet with your executives and learn about the business strategy and the long-term goals the company has, and how your product idea fits into this larger scheme.

You can use one or more of these tools to complement your analysis:

## SWOT

The SWOT analysis — Strengths, Weaknesses, Opportunities, Threats — is an easy framework to investigate a market and uncover possible gaps or opportunities. A SWOT analysis can be carried out for a company, a market, a product, or a customer.

## CONJOINT ANALYSIS

When you have a set of features or attributes and you would like to understand the relative value that customers place on each of them, and on possible combinations, conjoint analysis is a useful tool. It is an analytical tool, often used in brand development, and it allows to map the relative value customers place on a set of attributes.

For a detailed description of Conjoint Analysis see:

FURTHER READING

Merle Crawford, Anthony Di Benedetto, *New Product management*, McGraw-Hill, 2008

## BUY-A-FEATURE

Buy-A-Feature is a useful tool to understand the value people place on a set of features, and to understand how they make tradeoffs between them. It is usually considered a prioritization method, and can be applied in the discovery phase to understand what customers value more in a set of competing features.

Buy-A-Feature can be employed as a relatively quick method to evaluate a large set of features with multiple people, in a limited time. A quick way to set this up for discovery is to use a simple online tool for surveys like Surveymonkey.com. You can also run this in person with a group of users.

There are many examples online on how to run Buy-A-Feature, and for an explanation of the methodology.

FURTHER READING

Luke Hohmann, *Innovation Games*, Addison-Wesley, 2007

## OPPORTUNITY CANVAS AND BUSINESS MODEL CANVAS

If you have an existing product you are trying to evolve, the Opportunity canvas developed by Jeff Patton & Associates is a great tool to formalize your ideas:

http://jpattonassociates.com/opportunity-canvas/

If you are working on a new product or are trying to define a new market opportunity, then a more general Business Model canvas may be the right tool to use:

https://strategyzer.com/canvas

# DAYBREAKHOTELS

A REAL STORY

**DayBreakHotels** is an online platform that allows booking hotel rooms for day use in luxury hotels. It offers its services to business travelers looking for a rest stop during a long airport layover, or leisure customers interested in a high-end experience at top hotel brands, at a fraction of the regular cost.

Founded in 2012 in Italy and opened to the public in early 2013, DayBreakHotels operates today across Europe and the US with a network of high-end hotel chains and independent properties that include Marriott, Starwood, and Hilton. Simon Botto, CEO and original founder, had the idea during his MBA studies as he looked at pain points in the hotel industry and at the bad reputation that hourly hotels had. He was inspired by the concepts of the Blue Ocean Strategy and set off to reinvent the hotel business for day use.

This is an excerpt of an interview on January 4, 2017

*How did you get the idea?*

During my MBA I worked on a project focused on the hotel industry. I had had direct experience with day-use hotels since I started playing professional water polo when I was 14 years old. Our team would travel on Saturdays: fly somewhere in the morning, stop for a few hours at a local hotel to rest and prepare, play the game, go back to the hotel for a debrief, then fly back home in the evening. I realized that these hotels were often empty, especially the business ones outside of large cities. Occupancy was clearly a pain point.

As an adult, I became a lawyer and I often travelled for work spending nights in luxurious hotels. But I was rarely able to enjoy any of the amenities the hotels offered. Luxury hotels try to differentiate themselves based on the amenities they offer as well as their excellent service, but not many people are really able to take advantage of all these extra services. I thought, why not open the doors to luxury during the day, as well?

*What are the pain points of the hotel business?*

On average, hotels have an occupancy rate of about 65%, which means that about 35% of their rooms remain empty. This translates in about 2.5 billion rooms unsold every year. Considering only European luxury hotels, this is almost $50B in lost revenue.

These high-end hotels offer lots of extra amenities to earn their "stars" — from swimming pools, to gourmet restaurants, to spas. The problem is they don't have the right customers for these services. Guests check in at 8pm and check out the next morning at 9am. Both business and leisure travelers tend to be away from the hotel or busy with meetings during the day.

So, you have a business that sells only one thing (the room), and still has 35% unsold inventory. And it has a set of additional services that should be cross-sell, but in reality, it can't really cross-sell them because it does not have the right customers.

*What advantages does DayBreakHotels offer to hotels?*

All those are necessary paint points if you look at the hotel as a place for tourists. But we said, let's redefine the hotel concept and create the opportunity for hotels to get new customers, the right customers for the services available, in a new market with low competition.

If you are a hotel today, you are in a commodity market with super-high competition. Instead, I tell you: come with me in this other market, it's complementary to your core business, it's low-competition, and the customer you get from the day-use today becomes a customer for your core business tomorrow. If he or she doesn't become a core customer, it becomes a referral anyway.

*Are there any cons?*

The risk was the preconceived reputation. Everybody's fear was to become associated to the hourly hotel, either in terms of customer base or quality of hotel.

But you can disconnect from that idea, and continue to offer a service to couples, similarly to regular overnight hotels. If you think about it, besides business travelers, couples are probably a large customer segment of any hotels. I'm talking about formal couples, that often cannot afford luxury hotels besides an anniversary or an important vacation. We can offer them access to luxury hotels even without any traveling. Ours is a service that offers much more value than the regular overnight hotel, it gives you the same service at half the price. It gives you a service that was not available before, and an experience that maybe you could not afford otherwise.

### So, who's using your service?

I think we have two main customer segments. The first one is leisure, therefore couples, friends. In general, anyone who'd like to go to a hotel whose normal price is beyond reach, and would like to experience it. A room that usually cost $1,000 may be available for day-use for $200. They can say "let's go to the Ritz-Carlton at half price and in addition we get the spa". They can bring their spouse, a group of friends, whomever they like.

And we have another segment, the business traveler. This is potentially very large, we see a trend, but we don't know how big it is yet. The coworking industry (Wework, Make Offices, etc.) has raised $1B and a US study says that by 2020 about 40% of the working population will be freelance or solo entrepreneur. We expect to take a slice of that market. The day-hotel can be an alternative to a temporary office if you are a day traveler.

### You had this idea, then how did you build it?

When I first spoke with Flavio and Lorenzo [CTO and IT Director, respectively] they didn't want to meet with me. They thought it was yet another hotel reservation website. They said something like: "Look, find a job, because you are about 15 years too late."

But then we met in person, and I shared with them a concept I had drawn on a piece of paper. I used a pencil because I'm not good at Excel or PowerPoint. I just had a couple of sheets of paper, and we spoke about it. They loved the idea.

### How did you validate the idea, how did you know there was demand?

In truth, we set off without any market test. This came later. We started designing the system and we were convinced there would be demand. However, soon we realized that we needed someone who knew about the hotel business.

Through a friend, we met Michele, who had worked in the hotel industry for many years. He had personal contacts in hotels across the country. He did the first market test for us.

In two weeks, Michele called 50 hotels. He didn't even have anything to show, he just spoke on the phone. He described the idea and asked if they'd sign up for it. And most of the hotels said yes.

A few days later Michele joined our team.

*What did your first MVP look like?*

It was a basic website with a search page, a menu and a list of favorites. We didn't even break down by city. And there was no SEO (Search Engine Optimization). We, the four founders, worked together to build the MVP. Then, about five months later, we revamped the website adding support for SEO, with the help of an outside expert. And then again, the four of us, we built the mobile website.

*How did you launch?*

We launched in February 2013. Our site went live, and we thought that reservations would start pouring in. Instead, they we not coming.

The thing is, this is a new market, and it's a new service. People don't know it exists, and we need to educate them. Nobody has yet spent a big budget on a marketing campaign. We are basically creating a new market from scratch. This is the Blue Ocean concept.

For us, PR has been a great help. If you don't have money to spend on marketing and if you get the press to do marketing for you, it's very important.

*Do you use a methodology to prioritize your features?*

No… we don't even use Agile, not yet. Typically, we build wireframes, then we give them to our designer for the UI. We use internal testing and validation.

We are just starting to incorporate external customer feedback. We realize it's important, and our new UI/UX designer is really pushing for it. We use a prototype to get feedback, usually a wireframe, low-res.

I'd like at some point in the near future to have a product owner. It seems a logical step. Up until recently we didn't have the money to hire one. It wasn't core. We focused on building our engineering team and bringing new hotels in. Nobody on the team has specific expertise in product management. Not even a vice-vice-product owner.

*The biggest challenge now?*

I think it's finding the right people to grow the team.

Going through fundraising has helped me to clarify a lot of our business. Now I need to define the priorities, and bring in the right people. This translates in creating a good work environment, where people want to stay, and it means retention and value for the business.

Before moving into our new office, we worked in 450 square feet in my apartment, in a team of 13-14 people. It's easier to create a positive environment when you don't have money. The reasons people come to work are more aligned with the business needs. It's self-selection. There is low risk of getting people that come to work uniquely to make money, because you can't pay a salary.

Now we are looking for people who have the same spirit, and can integrate with the rest of the organization. In a job interview, anyone can fake it. You really need to see if that person can work with others. I prefer to collaborate on a project before hiring them.

# SYNTHESIZE YOUR LEARNINGS

Synthesizing information allows for making sense of all different data inputs collected during your Discovery and organize them into a coherent form. This allows for highlighting key insights from your research, identifying any gaps that require further analysis, and creating a concise presentation of your product idea to share with stakeholders, management, or your own team.

I'd like to share three tools I find useful with the teams I work with: the Mindmap, the Vision Statement, and the Product Innovation Charter.

## MINDMAP

A Mindmap is used to capture learnings, key assumptions, associated thoughts and ideas, and draw connections between them. It can be useful to jot down thoughts on a defined problem, document insights and different points of view. A Mindmap can be created "solo" or together with other team members. The end result is a visual representation of your Discovery on a specific topic, that you can save for later reference or share with others.

To create a Mindmap, follow these simple steps:

1) Relax, free up your mind, and find a quiet place where you can think.

2) In the middle of a piece of paper or whiteboard, write the main topic or problem statement. It can be just a word, or you can use the format: "How might we...." and fill the blanks with a concise statement that summarizes the main problem you are trying to solve. For example: "HMW democratize taxi rides to make them easier and cheaper?" — for an Uber competitor.

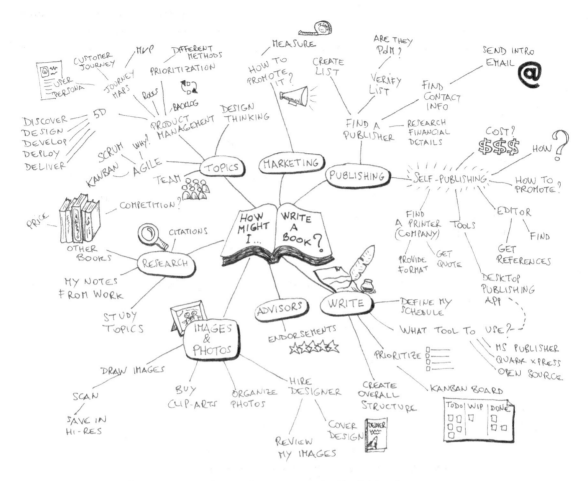

The initial Mindmap I created for this book

3) Write down the first thing that comes to mind and then draw a line to connect to the main topic. Write down the next thought, and connect it to the previous one, creating a sort of chain between connected thoughts.

4) Continue the chain of thoughts until you reach the end, then go back to the beginning and start a new chain of thoughts. A thought can be an idea, an insight you learned, a data point, a question you have not answered, or an assumption.

5) Once completed, highlight any major category or grouping, and create new connections between similar thoughts. Use different colors for these.

I find the Mindmap a useful tool that can be adapted to many different needs. You can use it not only to visually synthesize your Discovery learnings, but also for other purposes, for example to warm up the creative juices before an ideation session, to brainstorm ideas on your next career move, or to ideate topics for a speech you are invited to give.

## VISION STATEMENT

When working on a new product, you often need to find a succinct yet compelling way to communicate its value and your end goals. Maybe you are meeting one of your top investors in the elevator and only have 30 seconds to share your idea. Or you are hiring an external marketing firm to create an exciting advertising campaign and need to make sure the messaging is aligned with what your product does. Or you are hiring new team members to help with the product's development, and you need to rally them around your idea.

Whatever the reason, it all starts with a vision. The product vision paints the picture of what you are striving to achieve and the long-term goal for your product:

- What types of customers will you serve?

- What types of services will you offer?

- What value will you deliver?

- Why would anyone be interested in it?

SpaceX builds advanced rockets and spacecraft. Since 2002, it has been delivering satellites into space for commercial customers and payloads for NASA. SpaceX engineers were the first to introduce several innovations, including the ability for a rocket launcher to re-enter Earth's atmosphere and land back on the launch pad. Yet, for all its technical achievements, SpaceX's vision does not describe building the fastest, biggest, most advanced rocket. This is certainly part of what the company strives to do, but its long-term goals are more ambitious than that.

SpaceX wants to make humans a space-faring race. It wants to colonize Mars: *"SpaceX designs, manufactures and launches advanced rockets and spacecraft. The company was founded in 2002 to revolutionize space technology, with the ultimate goal of enabling people to live on other planets."[7]*

# THE POSITIONING STATEMENT

A Product Vision can be expressed in a multitude of ways. The Positioning Statemen (also called Problem Statement or Value Proposition Statement) is a useful framework to jot down the key elements of a Product Vision in a clear and concise statement.[8] It aims to answer the question: what customer problem (or market need) are you solving for?

This is not a long document. It's composed of one short paragraph succinctly describing what the problem is, who is having that problem, and the benefits offered by your solution. It should be framed from the customer's point of view.

FOR <who the target customer is>

WHO NEEDS <describe the customer's need or problem they have>

OUR PRODUCT IS <product category or brief description of the product>

THAT PROVIDES <key benefit>

UNLIKE <alternatives and competing products>

WE OFFER <unique differentiator and capabilities that address the needs>

## TIPS

I find it useful to write the Positioning Statement on an easel pad and post it on a wall to which the team can easily refer. Especially during the early phases of product ideation, I invite my team to refer to the Positioning Statement often to keep our minds focused on what we are trying to solve.

When you share your Product Vision with others, the best ways are visual and interactive, able to convey the vision and excite your listeners — an interactive presentation with video, an in-person skit, or a simulation of the problem you are trying to solve. These are much more compelling than a boring PowerPoint slide with a long page of text.

## FURTHER READING

Geoffrey A. Moore, *Crossing the chasm*, 1991

# PRODUCT INNOVATION CHARTER (PIC)

Another tool to document the business context for your product is the Product Innovation Charter (or PIC). You can think of it as a sort of business plan for your product. However, the PIC is intended for internal use and not for outside investors. It creates alignment between the product team, the executives, and other stakeholders for a common understanding of the business context in which the new product will operate.

Initially formalized in the 1990s by Merle Crawford, a 2007 study conducted by the PDMA (Product Development Management Association) found that 29% of firms have a formal PIC and 75% of the firms have some sort of new product policy (a derivation of PIC).[9]

The Product Innovation Charter is composed of four main sections:

1) **Background:** This includes market opportunities, customer needs, and technological breakthroughs.

2) **Focus:** Key strengths and opportunities you can leverage in terms of both technical and market dimensions. Value proposition and target customers.

3) **Goals and objectives:** These include both the short-term and long-term goals (profit, growth, market share, etc.) and the metrics you can use to validate your goals.

4) **Guidelines and metrics:** What you can measure to track progress towards timeframe, quality, cost structure, profitability, usability.

The PIC is also a good place to document the plan across the 5 Dimensions: how are you planning to tackle the Discover, Design, Develop, Deploy and Deliver stages? What kind of resources and activities will you employ? By focusing early on all 5 Dimensions and charting your plan for the entire product development process, you can start identifying gaps and additional resources you may need. You can include the 5D Canvas in your PIC.

FURTHER READING

Merle Crawford, Anthony Di Benedetto, *New Product management*, McGraw-Hill, 2008

# 5D CANVAS

Now that you have a Product Vision and an initial set of information about the customer needs and the opportunity, it's a good time to look ahead across all 5 Dimensions and begin thinking about the activities to do at each stage. As we discussed in chapters 4 and 6, there is a risk in approaching the product development process as separate, consequential phases (basically, Waterfall). Instead, it's better to think about your product development process as a whole, look across each Dimension and plan what you expect to do at each stage — even if at this point you don't have yet a clear idea of the specifics.

For example:

- If you expect your product to need a training manual to go with it you may want to plan how you can develop it (probably some activities in Discover, Design and Develop) instead of waiting for your product to be ready and then scrambling to put the training manual together.

- If you plan to Deploy your first release of the product to a specific segment (say "Soccer Moms"), you may want to make sure to identify the user needs and create features that can be useful for that segment (in Discover and Design).

- If you know that you will need a specific metric to track performance of your product once you Deliver, you may want to incorporate that metric early in your Design and Development activities.

Use the 5D Canvas to jot down your action plan and describe how you are going to bring your product to life. Having visibility into all the activities you need to do — even if at high level — allows for better planning and prioritization of the overall process.

To use the Worksheet, identify the following for each Dimension:

## Needs

These are activities, data points, and artifacts that you need to do, collect or create. For example: "Understand who my target customers are" in Deliver, "Implement a regression testing platform" in Develop, "training manual" and "customer support" in Deploy. Mapping these out early in the process and across all 5 Dimensions helps to bring clarity on what you need to do.

## Challenges

What obstacles or difficulties do you expect to have to satisfy the needs listed before? Having clarity on your challenges helps in finding ways to plan solutions and choose the right tools to solve them. For example, if you don't have clarity on who your target customers are or how to market to them, you may identify that as a challenge and list it under Discover (research potential customers), Design (understand who they are) or Deliver (measure results delivered).

## Tools

Based on the challenges identified before, what tools and activities can you use and do to solve them? You can refer to the other side of the 5D Canvas, "The 5 Dimensions of Great Products", for a list of suggested tools and activities for each Dimension. "Empathy Interviews" to learn about your customer needs, "User Personas" to define who your target customer is, or "Attend a training class" to learn more about Agile and Scrum.

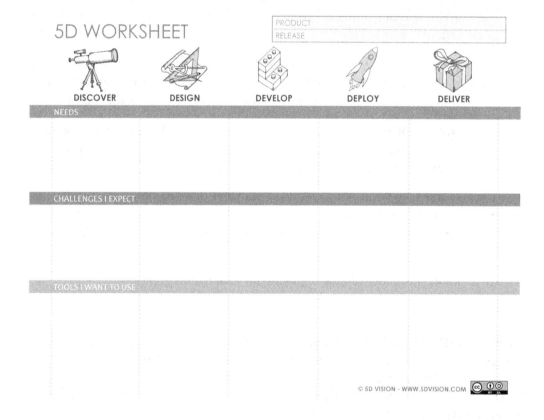

Download:
https://www.5dvision.com/docs/5d-canvas/

As you proceed through your product development process, you may revisit the 5D Canvas and update it with new learnings, add new challenges, and delete those you have already solved. In this sense, the 5D Canvas is a living document that accompanies you through your product journey. It provides a high-level map of how you plan to bring your product to life.

If you plan on developing your product in multiple releases, for example starting with an MVP and then following up with Version 2.0, etc., you can repeat the 5D Canvas using a different sheet for each release.

Refer to chapter 6 for more information on the 5 Dimensions of Product Management.

# REFERENCES

1. W. Chan Kim, Renée Mauborgne, *Blue Ocean Strategy: How to Create Uncontested Market Space and Make the Competition*, Harvard Business Review Press, 2015

2. "New product development", Wikipedia: https://en.wikipedia.org/wiki/New_product_development

3. Thomas J. Stanley, William D. Danko, *The Millionaire Next Door: The Surprising Secrets of America's Wealthy*, Taylor Trade Publishing, 2010

4. *Get Games from Goozex*, GamesRadar, 2007: http://www.gamesradar.com/get-games-from-goozex/

5. *5 Simple Ways to Stretch Your Gaming Dollars*, Wired, 2008: https://www.wired.com/2008/11/5-simple-ways-t/

6. Abbie Griffin and John Hauser, *The Voice of the Customer*, Marketing Science, 12, no.1, Winter 1993, pp 1-27

7. SpaceX website - http://www.spacex.com/about - December 8, 2017

8. Adapted from: Geoffrey A. Moore, *Crossing the chasm*, 1991

9. Merle Crawford, Anthony Di Benedetto, *New Product management*, McGraw-Hill, 2008

# NOTES

Building prototypes of a mobile app for a drone delivery system

# [8]

# DESIGN

Once you have identified an opportunity, a customer pain point, a gap in a market offering, or a technology breakthrough that you want to leverage, the next step is to design a solution. The goal of the Design phase is to narrow down to the best possible solution and build a working prototype that allows you to validate your hypotheses. This is the stage where business opportunity, human-centered design, and technology feasibility come together. This is also the stage where you may spend more time as you iterate on a series of prototypes and get feedback from end users to validate your hypotheses.

## USER PERSONAS AND THEIR JOURNEYS

The key to a successful launch of a new product is to understand who your target customers are, and what value your product offers them. Among the many tools available, the User Persona and the Customer Journey Map are great tools to document who you are building your product for, and what needs it tries to solve.

### USER PERSONAS

A User Persona helps to define who your target customers are. Instead of a generic segment of users, a Persona gives an identity to an individual person (real or fictional), helping your team identify and communicate more clearly the user needs.

User Personas are great tools to define who your customers are. A Persona is a representation of the goals and behaviors of a hypothesized group of users. In most cases, Personas are synthesized from data collected from user research and customer interviews.[1]

*A User Persona (or simply Persona) is a fictional representation of a customer of your product or service. It describes the motivations and needs of a typical user of your solution.*

You may have multiple Personas, especially if you identify different types of customers for your solution, with unique needs and expectations. Each type of customer may be represented by a specific User Persona. Sometimes your customers are from multiple user groups and you may have multiple user types interacting with your solution.

Take, for example, a taxi app that is used by both passengers and car drivers. Each user group has very different needs: passengers need to locate the nearest taxi and book a ride; drivers need to be alerted of a ride request, locate the requesting passenger, and manage the payments they received. Instead of talking about generic user segments, you can build a User Persona for a driver and for a passenger.

## How to create a Persona

To create a User Persona, start by selecting a person. This can be a real user of your product or a fictional one. The best User Personas come from interviewing, researching, and observing real people. You can even give them the name of the real person they represent. When building your Personas, be conscious of the different user groups and create a Persona for at least one user in each group (e.g. for taxi drivers and for passengers).

Well-crafted Personas don't just represent a generic group of people, but rather a specific individual (real or not). This Persona should have a name, a photo, details of his or her job, passions, and activities. And it should have a list of needs, motivations, or dreams.

Select someone who has clear motivations and specific needs, rather than just a generic customer.

Can you briefly describe this user? What actions, needs, and motivations are specific to this person?

See later in this chapter for a template of a User Persona.

## CUSTOMER JOURNEY MAPS

Customer Journey Maps are a visual representation of customer interactions with your business, product, online experience, retail experience, or any combination. These maps are developed from a customer point of view, designed to highlight how customers interact with your brand, product, services, and people. The more touchpoints you have, the more complicated — and useful — such a map becomes.

A Journey Map may focus on a specific interaction (e.g. a customer who visits your online store to buy a product, or a customer that calls customer service to solve an issue) or may take a broader view through several interactions (e.g. the decision to buy a new car may require an online search, a couple of visits to the dealer, a visit to the bank, etc.).

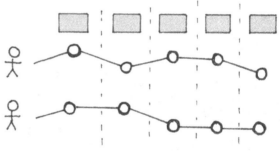

### Why use Customer Journey Maps

There are many reasons why Customer Journey Maps are useful. They can help to:

- Understand those moments of truth that have a significant impact on the customer experience.

- Identify gaps in the user experience when moving through the steps in the journey, interacting with different channels and touchpoints, or switching departments. Is the customer experience consistent? Are transitions smooth? Are there any gaps to fill?

- Create alignment among the team (and stakeholders) on the current pain points and the desired experience.

- Identify touchpoints and interactions among different actors. For example, in the case of car-sharing service Uber, the customer and the driver go through different experiences, yet they interact at multiple steps in the journey. A Customer Journey Map that overlaps the two actors helps identify the interactions and the respective points of view.

## Format of Customer Journey Map

There is no official format for a Customer Journey Map. A search on Google reveals that almost everyone uses a different format. It's not just a matter of graphical representation. A Customer Journey Map is specific to a business, a user context, a specific moment, and these make it unique. There are, however, common elements that guide the creation of a Journey Map and make it a great tool to understand the customer experience.

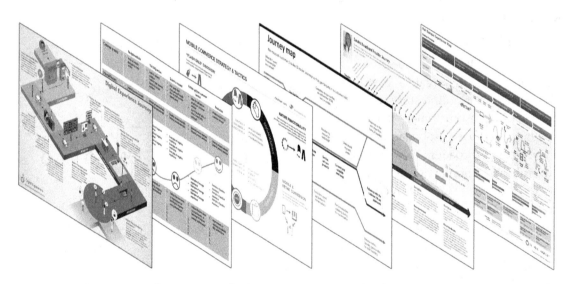

Several Journey Map examples found with a Google search

## How to create a Customer Journey Map

You can create a Customer Journey Map after you have identified the types of customers that use your product. You can then map out their experience through your product or service, identifying the activities they do and the emotional responses they have at each step of the journey.

## Scenario

Describe the scenario or context of the customer interaction you want to map out. What is the situation? What are the goals and expectations of the customer?

## User Persona

When building a Customer Journey Map, it is important to have clarity of who the "Customer" is. Rather than using a generic customer segment, use a specific User Persona. What actions, needs, and motivations are specific to this Persona?

You may have multiple User Personas, each one representing a different user type, with specific needs and activities. Create a Customer Journey Map for each of them to highlight different experiences with your product and identify possible intersections or gaps.

## Identify the touchpoints

Identify the touchpoints where the users interact with your product or service. A touchpoint is any point of interaction a user has with your business: a search page on the website, a checkout kiosk, a call to the customer service. These can be your current touchpoints if you are creating a Journey Map of the existing experience, or your future touchpoints if your product does not exist yet or you are planning an extension.

## Steps of the journey

Every journey starts with the first step.[2] To create a Journey Map, you need to identify the steps a user goes through in experiencing your product or service. The touchpoints identified above are a great start, but you may not want to stop there. You should highlight all the important steps the customers go through that are important in defining their experience. Some of these steps may be outside of your direct touchpoints: realizing they have a need, searching for information on Google, asking a passer-by for directions. By mapping these additional steps, you define the customer's journey in more clarity, and identify additional points of interaction with your customer that are not yet represented by current touchpoints.

A useful approach to define your steps is to think about the possible "moments that matter" a user may go through from the initial understanding of a need, to the resolution of that need with your product or service. Think With Google defines these as micro-moments and organizes them in four categories.[3]

Think about any of these "micro-moments" that are important for your customer's experience and add them to your Journey Map.

I-Want-to-Know Moments       I-Want-to-Go Moments

I-Want-to-Do Moments        I-Want-to-Buy Moments

Finally, the steps should be defined based on the customer's point of view, not your internal business processes. Once you have identified the possible steps in your customer's journey, sort them in linear progression. The usual approach is to place them on a horizontal line at the top of a whiteboard, leaving space below each step for the details of the Journey Map.

## Mapping the journey

Once you have identified the steps in your customer's journey, you are ready to complete the Journey Map.

Write down the name of the User Persona whose journey you are mapping, and then work out one step at a time, identifying the following information:

- **Goals and expectations:** What is your User Persona's intent at this step? What is it aiming to achieve? What does it need?

- **Touchpoints:** How does the User Persona interact with your product? What are the touchpoints at this step?

- **Activities:** What does the User Persona do at each step?

- **Emotions:** How does the User Persona feel at each step? What emotions does it show at each step? Is it happy, frustrated, curious, sad, excited?

## The "DURING", "PRE" and "POST" journeys

Typically, when building a Journey Map, we focus mainly on the core experience, the steps that customers go through while using the main features of our product or service (I call this the "DURING" phase). However, the user experience often starts before the actual interaction with the product or service, or it may extend past what the product offers.

I call these the "PRE" and "POST" phases. They identify steps in your customer's experience that take place before and after the core experience offered by your product. By looking at the "PRE" and "POST" experiences, you can identify other possible touchpoints and opportunities to extend your product for a richer and more satisfying experience.

Consider a bank branch. Customers may walk in to get help on all sorts of issues, from depositing a check to transferring money between accounts to opening a new savings account. You may be working at designing the branch of the future, finding ways to make the in-store customer experience simple and engaging. The in-store experience would be represented as the "DURING" phase in your Customer Journey Map.

However, the actual customer journey may begin well before the customer is physically inside your store. For example, you may want to consider these questions: why did they come there — what need were they trying to address? How did they find the store? These are decision points the customer went through (maybe unknowingly) before making the trip to the branch. You could identify and visualize these steps in your "PRE" phase.

Similarly, there could be opportunities to keep the customers engaged after they leave your store. How do they start using their new account? How do they get support? How do you keep them engaged with new offers? These can be steps in your "POST" phase.

### A Journey Map with multiple users

If you have multiple users that interact with each other, it's easier to start with individual journeys. Then, you can overlap the Journey Maps to identify the points of interaction. The maps should intersect where the different actors interact with each other. The result may be two or more lines that converge where the journeys intersect and diverge where the actors do activities independently.

See later in this chapter for a template of a Customer Journey Map.

**TRY THIS**

## Tip

I find it useful to start a Customer Journey Map on a whiteboard using Post-Its. This makes it easy to move things around and allows for team collaboration. Once the map is defined and agreed upon, digitize it with your favorite tool to preserve it for eternity and share it with stakeholders.

**A REAL STORY**

# THE SENSI THERMOSTAT

Emerson is a US company that offers a variety of products in the industrial and commercial markets, and is well known for heating and cooling systems. It owns some iconic consumer brands like InSinkErator and ClosetMaid, and has made a culture of innovation central to its strategy. The Sensi thermostat is a "smart" thermostat: it connects to Wi-Fi and can be managed remotely using an app on your phone. With the app, you can adjust the temperature of your home at any time, from anywhere; you can monitor the status and schedule of your heating/ cooling; and you can activate several options like remote lock of the keypad, on/ off setting of the system, and alerts.[4]

A few months ago, I wanted to replace an old thermostat with a smart one and spent hours on the Internet researching options and studying technical characteristics. There seemed to be a multitude of choices, with variations in design, price, and requirements. I was particularly concerned about the compatibility with my home system and ended up selecting the product that seemed the most promising. I bought a Sensi thermostat.

As soon as I purchased it, the anxiety kicked in. The idea of having a smart thermostat connected to Wi-Fi and managed through an app was cool, and I was excited by it. But I felt like I faced a wall of problems and unknowns on how to install it. What if, in the end, I have made the wrong choice and it would not work with my existing heating/cooling system? What if I don't have a "C" wire (the one that carries the power to the thermostat)? What happens if it doesn't connect to Wi-Fi?

Then I discovered the magic. The installation was a snap. Emerson had gone the extra mile to make the installation of its thermostat super-easy and to remove any barriers user may have. Its product team had spent time understanding the customer needs, and designing a product that is not only functional, but also easy to use. It went beyond building a product with a complete set of features, and strived to understand the user expectations and deliver an experience that is rewarding and enjoyable.

In my mind I could see the Customer Journey Map the product team must have created. It had a "DURING" phase focused on the core functionalities that you would expect from a product in its category: setup the daily schedule, Adjust the temperature remotely, See the status, Manage multiple thermostats on different floors, and more. All the things you could do with the thermostat during its daily use.

One of the biggest obstacles homeowners face in upgrading their thermostats is the installation. You must do it right, making sure to connect all wires in the right

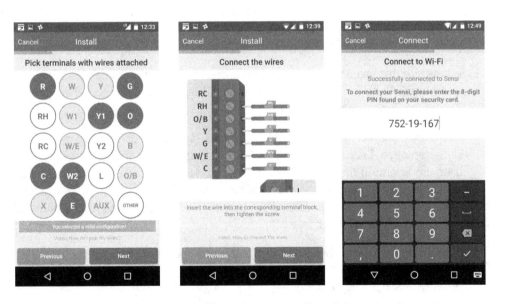

The Sensi app guides you through the installation of a
new thermostat removing most of the "unknowns" from
the process

order, and checking that the new thermostat is compatible with your home system (not all of them are). In reality, it's not much more complex than changing a light bulb, but the thermostat comes with a psychological weight: you are messing with your home's most complex system (the heating and cooling) and you feel the pressure of getting it right.

Thankfully, Emerson understood this, and it was apparent that the team had put a lot of effort in mapping out the "PRE" and "POST" phases of the customer journey, to simplify the installation process, reduce the anxiety, and provide support for any problem. The "PRE" phase must have included steps like Buying guide, Manage anxiety, Installation & configuration, Wi-Fi discovery, Wi-Fi router support. The "POST" phase must have included steps like Technical support, Maintenance, Checking power level, Upgrade or disposal, Share news and promotions.

When you unbox the new thermostat, the first thing you are invited to do is download the Sensi app. Here, through a series of screens, the system guides you step-by-step on how to disconnect the old thermostat, connect the new one, address problems with the "C" wire or other things, and finally power on the new system. It makes the installation a breeze, and because the app takes care of the details, I felt my anxiety vanish away.

That, until I finished the installation. As soon as I powered it on, I discovered that my new thermostat wouldn't work. In fact, it couldn't connect to Wi-Fi, no matter how many times I tried. For a Wi-Fi thermostat, it was failing on its main value proposition, and I felt frustrated and anxious.

Issues like this are unavoidable, and the best a product team can do is to assume that things will go wrong and identify ways to help customers solve their problems. Thankfully, Emerson was prepared.

The app offered an option to call and speak with a customer service representative. Frustrated and tired, I pressed the button and a couple of minutes later the agent on the phone had fully understood my situation and was ready to offer me a solution: mine was one of the few Wi-Fi routers that had a glitch and wouldn't work well with the Sensi thermostat. He offered me to upgrade my Wi-Fi router to a new model, for free.

I was completely taken aback. Not only was the Wi-Fi router not an Emerson product (in fact, it's a Cisco), but also they had no responsibility for its having a glitch in functionality. They could just have said "go buy a new router." Instead they offered the easiest solution for their customer, by replacing it for free.

Because I wanted to complete the installation that day, I declined the kind offer, learned that a different Sensi model worked fine with my router, and returned to the store to exchange the unit I had with the new model. In the end, the new model worked fine and finally connected in a breeze.

The product team had done its best to map out the user experience and have contingency plans for what could go wrong. They made all possible efforts to deliver a great customer experience, and not just build a good product.

# USING DESIGN SPRINTS FOR RAPID VALIDATION OF IDEAS

The idea behind a Design Sprint is to compress the time it takes to go from idea to validation for a specific problem to just a few days, rather than weeks or months. A Design Sprint brings together principles of Design Thinking and Agile, in a structured, time-boxing format. Originally designed by Google Ventures, the format of a Design Sprint can be adapted to take between three and five days, with the goal of ideating, designing, and prototyping a solution to a known problem.[5]

In my experience, a Design Sprint works well once the problem is understood, and the team has clarity on what is the general vision for the product. It can then use the Design Sprint to quickly validate one or more ideas in a short timeframe, get valuable feedback from end users, and then proceed to design the final solution. It shortens the time to validation and provides the team visibility on the key features that customers find valuable.

There are many resources available to learn more how to facilitate Design Sprints, including the Google Venture's website and a few books written by ex-Googlers.[6] These are all great resources, and they offer details on how to conduct the exercises.

When I started doing Design Sprints, I felt a bit confused by the variety of possible activities, and I wasn't sure which ones would fit my team's needs. I found it difficult to have undivided focus and commitment from my team members for an entire workweek, so I chose the compressed format of just four days, leaving the fifth as an optional day to continue refinement on prototypes as needed.

I also found that having a team warm-up exercise at the beginning of each day warms up the brain's creative juices and creates a stronger sense of team among the participants. Now, I always include a team warm-up exercise such as those described in the "Empower your team" chapter.

Over time, I have created my own schedule. This may not work for all situations, but it can be a good starting point if you want to get your feet wet with Design Sprints.

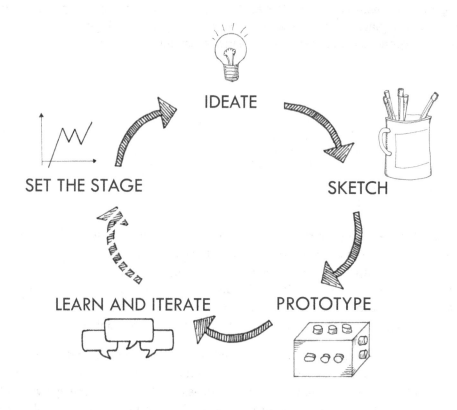

The phases of rapid validation using a Design Sprint

The infographic on the next page shows my customized schedule for running Design Sprints over four days, leaving Friday for further refinement of the concepts and additional prototype testing if needed (or just travel time back home for people coming in from different places). I have added team activities for morning warm-up, for team-building, and for retrospective at the end of each day. I have found that these activities help the team be more productive and cohesive.

You can download the four-day Design Sprint schedule from:

https://www.5dvision.com/docs/design-sprints/

TRY THIS

## Tips

Here are a few things I learned from my experience:

**Create a little competition within the team:** I learned that splitting the team in two sub-teams when working at prototypes makes the process more fun and

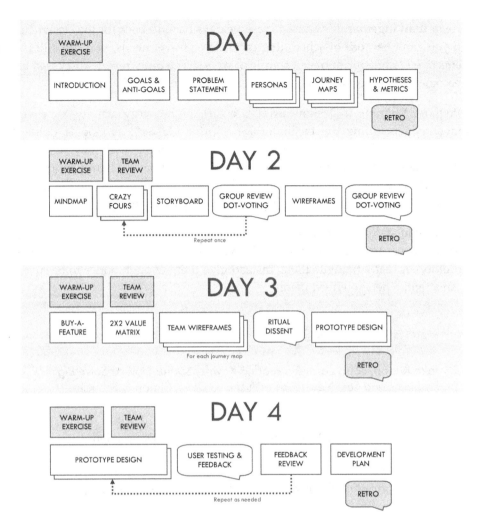

Customized schedule for 4-day Design Sprints[7]

generates two alternative sets of ideas that you can rally against each other. Of course, you need to have enough people on your team, but no more than eight to 10 to maintain your sanity.

**Warm up at the beginning of each day:** Do a creative warm-up exercise to get the mental juices flowing and create a stronger sense of team. For example, see the Spark Engine exercises or a few other ideas in the "Empower your Team" chapter. It's also useful to do a quick recap of the previous day. I like to have team members take turns at reviewing the work done the day before, so everyone feels more involved.

**Keep it all together:** It's better to reserve days back-to-back for the Design Sprint. If you can't because of scheduling conflicts or travel needs, you can still run an effective Design Sprint over a couple of weeks. The daily review discussed above becomes very important to refresh everyone's memory.

**Prepare:** Running a Design Sprint is a fast, high-energy activity for everyone involved, including the facilitator (or "Sprint Master", as Google defines it). Prepare the schedule of activities you plan on doing each day, and a brief description of how to run each exercise. Print it and have it handy or jot it down on a whiteboard — you will be grateful to have it once you are in the middle of an activity and you need to quickly organize the next one.

**Invite you stakeholders ahead of time:** Send invites to stakeholders, end users, or customers to test your work and give you feedback. Don't wait to have the prototypes ready to invite them, instead give them enough notice to be sure they can attend when you need them.

## FURTHER READING

Jake Knapp, John Zeratsky, Braden Kowitz, *Sprint: How to Solve Big Problems and Test New Ideas in Just Five Days*, Simon & Schuster, 2016

Richard Banfield, C. Todd Lombardo, Trace Wax, *Design Sprint*, O'Reilly, 2016

*The Design Sprint*, Google Ventures, http://www.gv.com/sprint/

# PRODUCT JOURNEY MAPS AND MVP

It is said that most initial releases of products are twice as big as they should be and that teams could shed some functionalities while still achieving the same objectives. But the reality is that it's very difficult to define what a real MVP is (Minimum Viable Product, discussed in the chapter 10). It's difficult to have both a broad enough vision of the product, and a detailed view of every feature at the same time, and use these to determine your minimum MVP.

Product Journey Maps solve these problems. They help visualize the long-term roadmap and define when each feature will be released; clarify what features are really needed in your initial release (clue: it depends on your objectives) and what features are less important and can be moved to a later time; and reveal the entire plan of your product for stakeholders and customers.

The Product Journey Map helps in maintaining focus on the MVP, even in the context of continuous pressure from stakeholders and customers to revisit priorities and add scope (I'm not saying you shouldn't do these, but the Product Journey Map helps in making the tradeoffs of any change visible to everyone). A side benefit of creating a physical Product Journey Map on a wall or whiteboard is that making changes to it becomes a visual activity — everyone sees it. It takes commitment and a shared understanding to move a card from a future release up to the MVP, or to add a new feature to an already planned release.

I was first introduced to the concept of Product Journey Maps during a lecture on product management several years ago.[8] It was Winter in frigid Minneapolis, but I felt energized by what I was learning. Since then, I have been a prophet of Product Journey Maps, using them for every new product effort and adapting the basic concept to suit the planning of different types of products and services.

Now that you get how excited I am about this tool, let's look at how it works.

## HOW TO CREATE A PRODUCT JOURNEY MAP

Like many things in life, your success depends on preparation. In my experience, preparation relies on understanding who the target customer is, what problem you are trying to solve, and the overall customer experience you intend to build. User Personas, Problem/Vision Statement, and Customer Journey Maps are useful tools to keep handy when planning to map your product's journey. It's also important for everyone on the team to be aligned on the general context of what you are trying to achieve, including business goals, key hypotheses, budget constraints, critical timelines, key partnerships or resources available, and technology opportunities. This is necessary groundwork to prepare for a Product Journey Map session.

At the beginning of the session, start with a creative warm up exercise as described in chapter 5 "Empower your team". After all, this is a creative activity — based on insights and data — but nonetheless creative, and having the right mindset and an active brain makes for a more productive session. A Mindmap can be another useful exercise to jot down on paper any initial thoughts, questions, or assumptions you already have on the topic, and keep it visible for reference as you continue the work.

## Identify the key steps of the journey

When you are ready, convene your team around a whiteboard or an empty wall, and start creating your Product Journey Map together.

The first step in creating a Product Journey Map is to identify the steps (or stages) of your customer experience. These can be represented by the different stages a customer goes through when using your product. If you have built a Customer Journey Map, you have probably already identified all the important steps.

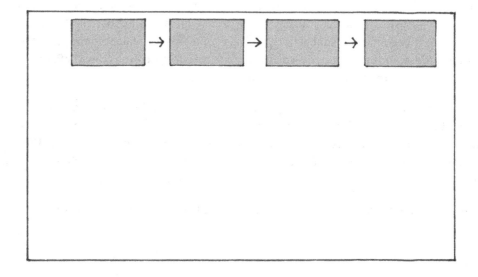

For example, for an online ecommerce website, your customer most commonly goes through the following stages: Search for products, View Product, Add to Cart, Manage Cart, Checkout, Register/Login, Print Receipt, and Track Order.

## Brainstorm a set of features for each step

For each of the steps in your map, jot down the list of features you'd like to build.

These are activities customers will do at each step. Write each activity on a separate feature card. For example, for the step "Search for products", customers may want to find products by category, by publisher, by price, or sort products using a variety of criteria. Each of these options can be represented as a feature card in your map.

For the first pass, I prefer keeping this at the "Feature" level as using smaller User Stories may be too granular. But you can test different methods until you find the right level of granularity that works for you.

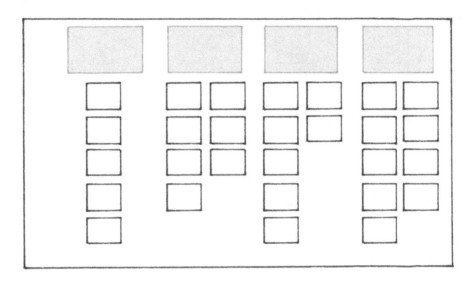

I also find it to be good practice to write the features as actions (verbs) and from a customer's point of view. For example, write "Pay with credit card" rather than "Credit card payments". It highlights the specific action the user does, and it's another subtle reminder that what we build should deliver value to a customer.

## Prioritize the most important features first

Once you have your list of features defined, you need to prioritize those that are most important to deliver the intended customer experience and most value to your customers.

If there is a feature that must be there otherwise nothing else works in your product, you may want to identify that as a high priority. If you need to validate a new concept, you may prioritize features that help you test your ideas. In any case, this is the time to decide what gets built first in your MVP, and what can wait. This is also the time to be critical of what gets prioritized and what doesn't, depending on the specific goals you are trying to achieve. For different prioritization methods, see the next chapter.

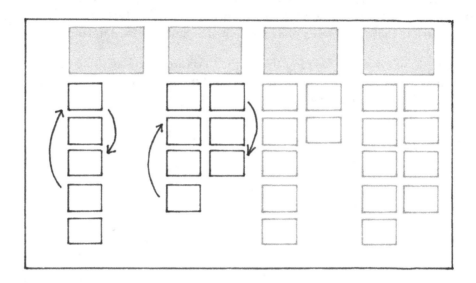

Once you have identified the priority for each feature card, move those that have a higher priority to the top, the others towards the bottom.

## Define the initial release

Now, draw a horizontal line across your map. This line represents your MVP boundary. Identify any feature card that does not belong to the MVP and move it below the line. The lower its priority, the lower it goes.

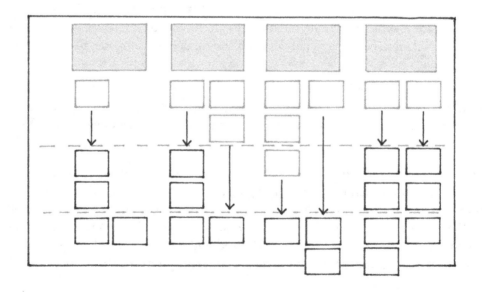

TRY
THIS

## TIP

I like to start by moving all the features below the MVP line, so that the top section is empty. Then, I make a conscious effort at moving those that I believe should be in the MVP back above the line, one by one. Moving a feature card up requires agreement across the team, and therefore a commitment to building it for the MVP. For each feature we want to move up I ask the team: *"Do we really need this for the MVP?"* and I move it up only if we agree on it. Everything that doesn't raise to the top section remains below for a future release.

## Identify additional releases and visualize your roadmap

You may draw additional horizontal lines to further divide your features across multiple releases. The feature cards above the MVP line define those that you have prioritized high enough and determined as critical for your MVP release. Those between the lower lines are the features that belong to future releases. Once finished, this provides a visual representation of your roadmap spanning multiple releases of your product. Stakeholders and customers can quickly glance at any release and understand what features will be available and when.

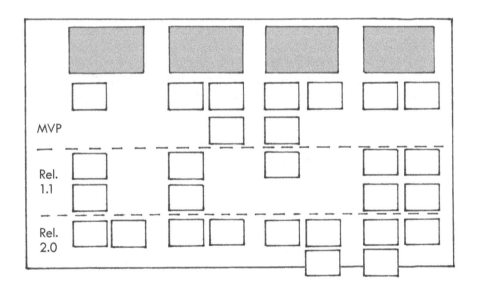

Congratulations, you have built your Product Journey Map!

## TIPS

When brainstorming with your team, make sure to generate as many features as possible. Some of these may be feasible, others may be far off in the future or seem unachievable. Make sure everyone feels included in the activity. Then, be surgical in deciding what moves up for the MVP and what moves down. You want to make your MVP as small as possible. The rest of the map provides the long-term view of your product.

When mapping out the plan for an MVP using a Product Journey Map, you can complement the list of features with a list of questions or hypotheses you'd like to validate. Your requirements become assumptions. Instead of starting from a point of knowledge, you start from a point of discovery and inquiry. Instead of building something, your goal is to validate your assumptions.

Those that go in the MVP are hypotheses that are critical to understand the validity of the product idea. Mapping out the hypotheses and their relative importance, gives the team focus on where to spend time and energy to validate the important questions and hypotheses, and provides clarity on what to postpone to a later study.

## FURTHER READING

"How Product Journey Maps can help planning your next MVP",
https://www.5dvision.com/post/using-product-journey-maps-to-plan-your-product-mvp/

Jeff Patton, *User Story Mapping: Discover the Whole Story, Build the Right Product*, O'Reilly Media, 2014

# PROTOTYPE, PROTOTYPE, PROTOTYPE

The cost of building a product and the risk of making the wrong choices grow higher over time. Building prototypes and testing with end users reduces the risk of investing in the wrong idea. As a product manager, you should have clarity of the key assumptions and hypotheses underlying your product idea, and validate as frequently as possible with end users or potential customers. This is an iterative process, starting with rough or low-fidelity prototypes, and adding details and variations over time.

## BUILD PROTOTYPES

When you have an idea of what you'd like to build, and before you commit to spending resources on developing your final product, you should build a prototype and test it with the end users. Prototypes are a great way to get feedback from prospective customers and various stakeholders early in the product development cycle without too much of an upfront investment. They help to validate what is important for your customers, understand if the idea delivers value to the end users, and test your product's customer experience throughout the journey.

Simply put:

*A prototype is an early version of your product that allows you to test with end users and validate key assumptions on value delivered, design, functionality, and customer experience*

There are two key elements to a successful prototype:

**Validate hypotheses:** You should have clarity on what you need a prototype for. What key hypotheses do you need to validate (or disprove)? Define the key hypotheses, and then build a prototype that helps you learn about those. You may need to build different prototypes to test different hypotheses.

**Interact with a working model:** A prototype should be a working model of your product. The key to a good prototype is that the user needs to be able to interact with it. If someone is not able to interact with it, then it is a presentation not a prototype, and you are probably not learning much from it. Think about the difference between a sketch of a website on a piece of paper versus a series of wireframes that the users can flip as they navigate from one page to the other. The former would be a concept diagram, the latter a low-fidelity prototype that is quick to build and lets you learn about the key elements of your user experience.

A prototype can be built in a variety of manners:

- **Digital:** A digital representation of your product, app, or website. This could take the form of a 3D model, a working mockup, or just a simple wireframe built using interactive tools like Adobe InDesign or Balsamiq.

- **Physical:** A simulation of the customer experience built using Legos, cardboard, wood, or other materials. This can be a small-scale model (e.g. like the wooden model of a new building that architects put together) or a full-scale simulation of the end product (e.g. creating a new retail store experience in a test location — or warehouse — that you can easily change and adapt while getting feedback from real customers).

- **Walkthrough:** Acting-it-out simulation of the customer experience. Take your users through the intended experience you'd like to provide and observe what they do and how they interact with your prototype, e.g. a walkthrough prototype for a website could be a set of screens drawn on paper, one sheet per screen, with the users flipping to the next screen for each action they take.

There is no right or wrong method, and you should choose the one that best suits your needs depending on the type of product you are building, and the type of feedback you are seeking.

## DEFINE YOUR HYPOTHESES

As mentioned before, it's important to have clarity on the underlying hypotheses that can make your product work or determine its failure. Before you build a prototype, or an MVP, you should identify a list of hypotheses you need to validate. The idea is to define a number of hypotheses, prioritize them, and then run experiments to validate the hypotheses.

A great tool to structure and document hypotheses is the Test Card developed by Strategyzer.[9] The Test Card is a physical card that structures a hypothesis in a precise format. The Test Card allows to define not only the hypothesis you want to test, but also how you are going to measure it and what needs to be true to validate (or invalidate) the hypothesis.

A Test Card is structured as:

We believe that: <your hypothesis>

To verify that, we will: <your experiment>

We will measure: <metrics to look at>

We are right if: <expected results>

You can create as many Test Cards as needed, one for each hypothesis. Then put these cards in your Product Journey Map so that you can properly prioritize the activities to perform to validate each of the hypotheses.

### FURTHER READING

Alexander Osterwalder, Yves Pigneur, Gregory Bernarda, Alan Smith, Trish Papadakos, *Value Proposition Design: How to Create Products and Services Customers Want*, Wiley 2014

# PROTOTYPING A RETAIL USER EXPERIENCE

You can use prototypes of various forms to test different aspects of your product or service. For example, a few years ago my team and I were building a concierge app for a retail service company. The app would allow walk-in customers to sign up and get a spot in the queue with no need to wait in line for their turn with an associate. We built wireframes and tested the functionality of the app and its UI. We drew prototypes on paper so that we could change them on-the-fly based on feedback from our users, and tested multiple iterations in one session. These early prototypes helped us refine the functionality of the app.

However, we were not sure how to manage the physical aspects of the user experience in the store, for example the interaction between our store associates and the customers when a spot became available.

Instead of waiting to release the app in the real stores and observe how the associates used it, we decided to build a mock-up of the store in our office and prototype the user experience for both associates and customers. It wasn't anything fancy - using just a large room, a few tables and chairs, we setup a basic simulation of the retail space in our office. We were mostly interested in understanding the flow of people and their interaction with the digital app.

We then invited some fellow employees and assigned them different roles. We asked them to act out the customer experience of entering the store, signing up on the app, and then waiting for the next available associate.

By seeing how people interacted with the app and the surrounding space, we identified several flaws in our concept, related not to the app itself, but to how we expected our store associates to interact with customers. For example, when an associate became available, we had initially expected that he or she would walk around the store looking for the next customer in line. The associate could see the name of the next customer pop up on the app, and they could just call the customer by name. But shouting the customer's name around a large store was not perceived as either professional or friendly.

This and other insights gave us the spark to think about other ways to identify and locate the customer, including having their photo displayed on the employee's device, or sending them a text message. We would not have caught these flaws had we not simulated a walkthrough of the physical experience. It didn't require a huge investment to organize this test, but it saved us from building the wrong product based on flawed assumptions.

# REFERENCES

1.  Source: Wikipedia - https://en.wikipedia.org/wiki/Persona_(user_experience) - Pulled Feb 15, 2017

2.  Adapted from Lao Tzu's proverb "A journey of a thousand miles begins with a single step"

3.  Source: "Micro-moments" https://www.thinkwithgoogle.com/collections/micromoments.html - Think with Google https://www.thinkwithgoogle.com/

4.  This story is based on the personal experience of the author and information available on the Emerson website. For more information on the product, refer to https://www.emerson.com/en-us/commercial-residential/sensi and https://www.youtube.com/watch?v=aFu-iDK3quQ

5.  Google Ventures - http://www.gv.com/sprint/

6.  Jake Knapp, John Zeratsky, Braden Kowitz, *Sprint: How to Solve Big Problems and Test New Ideas in Just Five Days*, Simon & Schuster, 2016

7.  Adapted from Richard Banfield, C.Todd Lombardo, Trace Wax, *Design Sprint*, O'Reilly, 2016

8.  Jeff Patton, *User Story Mapping: Discover the Whole Story, Build the Right Product*, O'Reilly Media, 2014

9.  Source: Strategyzer: http://blog.strategyzer.com/posts/2015/3/5/validate-your-ideas-with-the-test-card and https://strategyzer.com/

WORKSHEET

# USER PERSONA

**HOW TO USE THIS**

Describe in detail a particular user of your product. What are his or her needs and motivations? Prepare a Persona worksheet for each type of user you have.

Photo or avatar

NAME

OCCUPATION / ROLE

OTHER NOTES

ABOUT ME

MY MOTIVATIONS AND GOALS

MY NEEDS AND PROBLEM-TO-SOLVE





Download: https://www.5dvision.com/docs/user-persona-template/

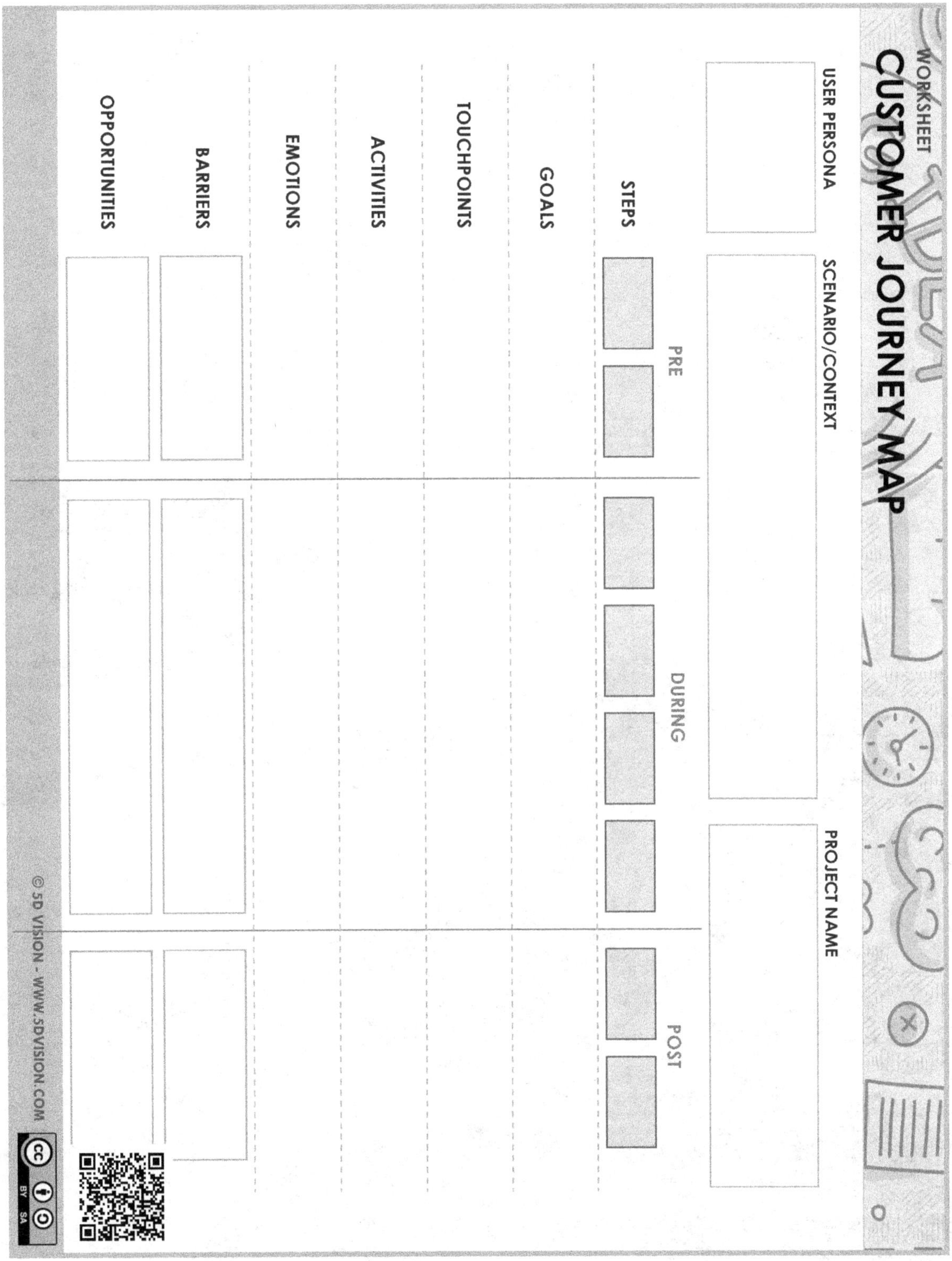
WORKSHEET
CUSTOMER JOURNEY MAP
USER PERSONA
SCENARIO/CONTEXT
PROJECT NAME
PRE
DURING
POST
STEPS
GOALS
TOUCHPOINTS
ACTIVITIES
EMOTIONS
BARRIERS
OPPORTUNITIES
© 5D VISION - WWW.5DVISION.COM
CC BY SA

Download: https://www.5dvision.com/docs/customer-journey-map-template/

Face-to-face collaboration is the most efficient way for teams to coordinate their work

# [9]

# DEVELOP

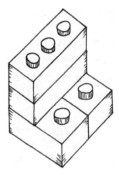

## THE DAILY TORNADO OF DEVELOPMENT

We live in a world of constant change. Even inside our companies, things are never static, and we hardly have the time to complete one activity before being asked to work on the next. We are bombarded with input from every direction: management, customers, investors, social networks, media. Across the organization, anyone can submit a "ticket" and send a request for a new development to the team. The Sales and Marketing teams are always fighting a battle with time, and demand that their needs be satisfied first — after all, they say that the customers come first. The CEO stops by the office and asks to put on hold everything we are doing and begin working on the latest idea. And finally, there is the long list of capabilities that we believe fit with the strategic direction or "vision" that the company has established, but we hardly have the time to work on any of the new capabilities. Our team is in a constant struggle to build the next urgent thing.

Sound familiar? I have experienced these situations with numerous product teams across a variety of industries. The teams struggle to keep up with a mounting list of demands coming from anywhere in the organization, with conflicting priorities, loosely described requirements, and last-minute emergencies. To make sense of all this, the developers try to multitask and work long hours, only to find themselves submerged even more in the daily tornado of things to do. The result usually falls into one of three categories:

**The team burns out**: Working in bursts all the time is not sustainable over the long term. The team members understand that there must be a better way of doing things, and at some point, they realize that the only way to get out of the daily tornado is to get out of the company and find a better place to work.

**The product fails**: After working long hours and trying to satisfy everyone across the company, the team has been able to deliver a bit of this and a bit of that, but none of the big and important capabilities that would make the product stand out in the market. Once deployed, the product is received with mild interest from customers, who quickly request changes and new capabilities — adding to an already long list of things to do.

**The technical debt kills the company**: In a constant struggle to keep up with customer requests and build the next important thing, the product becomes a sort of bread pudding of capabilities — it may taste good, but you have no idea what's inside. As the team keeps adding new features, it forgoes testing, performance, or architectural evolution. After some time, the product becomes so complex that it's difficult to update and improve. Changes become increasingly difficult, and no one has the time to fix the overall architecture. In the meantime, some competitor — who is nimbler and more focused — has stolen the market. At some point, the company struggles to keep up, loses market share, and runs out of money.

Things don't need to be this way. You can build a great product, keep your stakeholders happy, and empower your team for the long run. It requires changing how the organization sees the development activities.

## CLOSING THE GAP BETWEEN TECHNOLOGY AND BUSINESS

The development team should not be a black box that is handed an ever-changing list of requirements and expected to complete them as quickly as possible (and perhaps penalized if it doesn't do it on time). The business and the technology teams should work in partnership to understand the context of the project, to define the relative priorities, and to negotiate the roadmap and possible trade-offs of scope changes.

Empowering the development team is one of the pillars of great products, as we discussed in chapter 5.

The entire organization needs to work together towards delivering the most value to its customers, rather than trying to maximize the personal return of each department. Individual priorities should be replaced with overall customer value, represented by a unified Product Backlog that is constantly updated and prioritized. Avoid multitasking and working at too many things at once. Instead, prioritize your work, impose WIP limits (Work-in-Progress), and visualize your bottlenecks to maximize the flow of work and speed up delivery.

Products should be built in increments, validated with customers at every step, and updated when needed. Rather than building the whole thing at once and hoping to get it right, take it through incremental steps and aim for a Minimum Viable Product (MVP). By infusing a culture of Agility (see chapter 4), you minimize the risk of building the wrong thing, improve the efficiency of resources, and get feedback along the way. After all, if you need to change something, it's better to do it as soon as possible, rather than waiting to have completed the development.

The development team needs to have the space and time to implement the right practices and build a robust architecture, rather than struggle for air every day. Today's practices of DevOps, ATDD, CI/CD, allow teams to focus on quality of their work, limit technical debt, and build products on top of foundations that are robust, reliable, and designed for the long run.

# THE PRODUCT BACKLOG

All work starts with a Product Backlog. This is the list of all features, enhancements, and bug fixes that you intend to work on. The goal of the Backlog is to keep track of all the work that needs to be done, and to focus on the most valuable work first. It is maintained and prioritized by a product manager, who is responsible for its content and for setting the relative priorities between items. The product manager should be empowered to have the ultimate word on what goes into the Backlog and what is prioritized.

The Backlog is a public document that can be shared with the rest of the team and with stakeholders. The product manager updates the Backlog as often as necessary. Other team members may contribute, but the product manager remains solely responsible for it.

# WORKING WITH A PRODUCT BACKLOG

## Where does a Backlog come from?

It all starts with the vision. Setting a compelling vision for what the product will be allows the team, the organization, and your end users to rally behind the idea and support its development. A reality of our world is that it takes money to build things, so you also need to secure a budget — from your department, your investors, or your own portfolio if you are bootstrapping a new company.

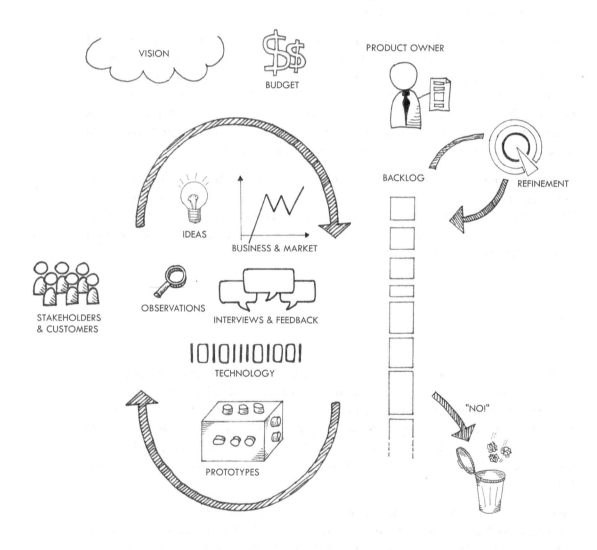

The origin of a Product Backlog

Creating and maintaining a product Backlog is then a continuous cycle of learning (from the market, your customers, and your own discovery), refinement (measuring the outcomes of your effort and adapting your plan), and prioritization (making sure the most important tasks are at the top).

The learning comes from multiple sources including your own ideas and explorations, business and market opportunities, observations and interviews with customers, feedback received from the end users of your product, technology breakthroughs, and feedback collected from testing prototypes of your product. Each one of these activities can be a source of new input to the Backlog or can drive changes to existing Backlog items (e.g. you may discover that a feature you deemed important is not considered so by your end users and instead something else may be more important).

## Continuously refining your Backlog

The Backlog is not a long document of requirements that describes every single detail of everything the system should do. Nor is it a static list of work items that is compiled once and then handed to the development team to execute (in the old days that was called a Business Requirements Document — or something similar). The Backlog is a living document that, at any point in time, represents the work to be done. As the team learns new details from the market, receives feedback from users, validates hypotheses, and even deploys parts of the product, the work to be done is adjusted, updated, and expanded (or reduced). Refinement and prioritization of the Backlog are continuous activities.

A feature may be moved down in the Backlog if it has low priority and may be revised later. Some of the work items may be eliminated entirely if no longer needed. Others may be re-prioritized as the team learns what delivers the highest value. Some work items may be expanded, compressed, or split in multiple parts (e.g. splitting User Stories or breaking down a Feature in User Stories). New work items may be added to expand the scope of the product or include capabilities not planned initially.

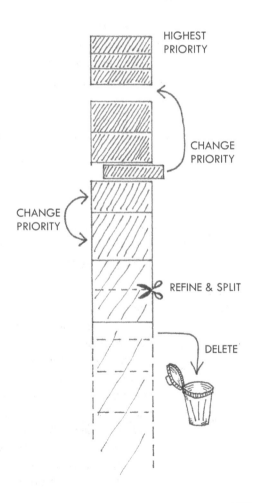

HIGHEST PRIORITY

CHANGE PRIORITY

CHANGE PRIORITY

REFINE & SPLIT

DELETE

## Say "No!" to keep your Backlog in check

Almost half of the features built into new products are rarely used, so it's extremely important to validate and prioritize appropriately the work that needs to be done. One of the most important skills a product manager must possess is the ability to say "No" and remove items from the Backlog. Since the product manager is the key "owner" of the product, he or she is also responsible for what is included in it, and what is dropped. And that also means being able to say "No" if you believe a feature request would not deliver value or would be much lower in priority than other things you intend to build.

At times, saying "No" can be uncomfortable. A customer may request a feature or ask you to include it in the MVP of your product. Someone on your Sales team may call you and say, "I really need this additional feature to sell the product to XYZ customer." Your CEO may stop by your desk and declare what they think should be done next.

Having a healthy conversation with your stakeholders is always important and hearing their input can give a useful data point to evaluate priorities. However, when the Backlog is driven by the loudest or strongest voice in the company, the product manager becomes unempowered, the Backlog is subject to the whim of the moment, and the development team risks becoming overworked and churning out features that deliver little value. Empowering the product manager to say "No" requires alignment across the entire organization.

# THE FAILURE OF EVER-CHANGING PRIORITIES

Several years ago, I worked for a CEO who was a micro-manager and who needed to maintain control of everything happening in his company. From a product development perspective, he was a disaster. He was convinced that the struggles his company faced could be solved by a few quick changes to the product. The reality was that the business had to reinvent itself. The world was changing, the customer needs were changing, and the business had to adapt with a new product offering and a pivot in strategy. Instead of maintaining the focus on the larger vision, he kept responding to the daily pressure of slowing sales, and the latest idea from Google's SEO newsletter (Search Engine Optimization). He frequently changed priorities, asking to work on the next important thing before we had finished the previous one.

As product manager, I felt unempowered and frustrated by the lack of progress we were making. It was a constant struggle between building a better product and responding to the CEO's latest requests. The Backlog ballooned, the team felt overworked, and the company was going nowhere as sales stagnated and customers fled.

At one point, we devised a strategic pivot that would make our offering more appealing to a large segment of customers who were unhappy with our current offering. After weeks of planning and a management offsite, we had everybody onboard. My team was ready to begin working on it. Then the CEO spoke with a new SEO consultant, who provided us a list of improvements for the "old" product. The CEO was, once again, convinced that the SEO would "fix" everything, and so he demanded daily updates on SEO improvements. Our focus was gone, and the important strategic pivot was forgotten.

To his credit, Google had recently made headlines for recent changes to its search algorithm (the so-called "Panda" update), and the impact to search results it had for many online businesses.[1] The irony was that our website was losing customers every day. It didn't matter if we were able to acquire a few more thanks to better SEO, until we had a better value proposition that would keep them there. Working at the SEO improvements felt like putting more gasoline in a car with deflated tires: no matter the effort, we would not go far.

My team and I managed to develop and launch a few important product improvements despite the cacophony of changing demands. These wins came at high cost in terms of energy, commitment, and time. But, despite all the effort, the product's performance in the market didn't improve much.

I learned at that time that, as a leader, empowering your product manager to make decisions on the Backlog and its prioritization is critical to the success of a product. Certainly, the product manager cannot act in a void — he or she needs to have context, resources, access to customers. The product manager should work with the CEO, the sales department, and other parts of the organization to define a product strategy that maximizes value for the company and its customers. And then that person should be empowered to execute the product strategy. Smaller things, urgent updates, and fixes can find a place in the development activities, but the focus should not steer away from the overall strategy.

A side note, today I would have approached this differently, by visualizing all the work with a Kanban board with multiple swim lanes. One swim lane dedicated to the "strategic work" and the other to "SEO updates". And I would have negotiated capacity allocation of development resources across all lanes. That would have created alignment across the organization and transparency on the work being accomplished, and possibly have avoided the personal struggles my team and I faced daily. But this is a different story...

## STRUCTURE OF A BACKLOG

The Backlog may contain a few dozen or hundreds of work items. Each item represents a new capability, feature, or fix that the team intends to work on. Work items are called Product Backlog Items, just a fancy name to highlight that the item belongs to a Product Backlog.

### Types of work items

The Backlog includes everything the team needs to work on. Some of the work items are provided by the product manager and describe new work for the product. Other work items may be provided by the development team itself and describe improvements it needs to make to its own development process. At any point in time, a Backlog may include a combination of the following:

- **New features and capabilities:** For example, adding a new functionality to your website.

- **Bug fixes:** Somehow defects keep showing up despite our best effort and need to be fixed.

- **Quick changes:** Updating the existing product with small, quick fixes, like changing the logo, updating the text on a page, or adding support for a new type of customer.

- **Architecture enablers:** Work on the overall architecture of the system, including infrastructure, automated testing, performance improvements, security, data repositories. A good product is built upon a solid foundation. The team needs to dedicate time to maintain and update the foundation over time or risks incurring technical debt.

- **Team improvements:** Changes to processes, tools, and resources that the team needs to become more effective (often highlighted during a team's retrospective). For example, if the team needs to spend time researching a new technology, the Backlog should contain a "research spike" to reserve capacity and properly prioritize this activity.

Giving priority only to new features and capabilities, leaving behind bug fixes and architectural improvements, creates the long-term risk of a product that is not working properly or whose architecture becomes fragile (read how a company realized it had this problem and how it overcame it in the BookingBug story later in the chapter).

On the contrary, focusing time only on fixing bugs and improving the architecture, doesn't allow the product to grow with new features and capabilities, lagging behind competitors that may be faster in growing their products (you don't want to become the next Blackberry, and risk missing out on an important innovation that is instead capitalized by a faster and nimbler competitor — Apple, in this case).

The job of a product manager is, therefore, to understand the importance of any of these work items and properly prioritize them in the Backlog.

## Description of an item

Work items in the Backlog should be expressed from the point-of-view of the value they deliver to the business and to your customers. The most common information you need to save for each item includes:

- **Name of the item:** Short, at-a-glance descriptive name for the new feature, activity, or fix

- **Description:** Detailed description of what this work item is supposed to do, offer, or fix

- **Benefit:** Who's going to benefit from this work item, and what benefits they will gain

- **Priority:** A priority value assigned to this item relative to everything else

- **Requirements:** Any technical requirements you may have. For example, length of a password, minimum performance, support for security, etc.

One common way to document work items is to use the User Story format. We'll see that later.

Work always starts with the items at the top, those with the highest priority. These are also more refined in terms of description, details, requirements. Instead, the items at the bottom may be very loosely detailed, often with just a single line describing an idea and nothing more. These items will be refined when they rise near the top.

## Number of items

You may set guidelines in terms of how many items to keep in your Backlog or for how long. Usually, having hundreds of items that never move, or items that sit in the Backlog for years, is not very useful. By the time you can get to work on these items, the business strategy, the market dynamics, the customer needs, the technology, or several other factors may have changed, rendering these items no longer needed or valuable.

Set your own guidelines and, for example, remove items from the Backlog if they are stale for more than six months (or whatever period is reasonable for your organization or project) or if you have more than 50-100 items (or whatever number your team is likely to work on in the next 6-12 months).

## VISUALIZE YOUR WORK ON A TEAM BOARD

The Kanban Board (also called just "Board" or "Team Board" when used to track progress within a Sprint) is a useful tool to visualize work in progress and track what has been completed. It can be customized to fit your organization's specific needs, and it's usually drawn on a whiteboard or using a digital tool.

In its basic implementation, it has three columns, each representing a stage in which a work item can be during development:

- **TO DO:** All the items in the Backlog, with the prioritized ones at the top. This may not necessarily be the entire Backlog, but only the portion the team has committed to working on in the next few weeks. For example, in Scrum this takes the form of the Sprint Backlog for the current Sprint. Items may wait in the Backlog column until they are ready for development.

- **WIP – WORK-IN-PROGRESS** (or simply DOING): Items that the team is currently working on. To maintain focus and reduce multitasking, it is good practice to limit the number of items in progress to just a few at a time, finding a reasonable limit that works for your team.

- **DONE:** Finally, the items that are completed and fully tested are moved to the "Done" column. This column summarizes, at quick glance, all the work the team has accomplished so far.

### Customize your Kanban board

The idea of a Kanban board is to provide a general framework to visualize the flow of work and keep track of status. In practice, the Kanban board's columns are customized to represent your specific team's workflow steps. A software development team may have a "Test" column and possibly a few more steps like "Ready for QA", "In QA", "Staging", etc. A Google search for "Kanban Board Examples" shows many ways the Kanban board can be customized to suit your project's or organization's specific needs.

In writing this book, I created my own Kanban board composed of four columns: "Backlog", "Work-In-Progress", "Editing & Review", "Done". My Backlog was the list of chapters, stories, and images I needed to work on to create the book. I moved to "Work-In-Progress" one chapter at a time and maybe some other smaller task,

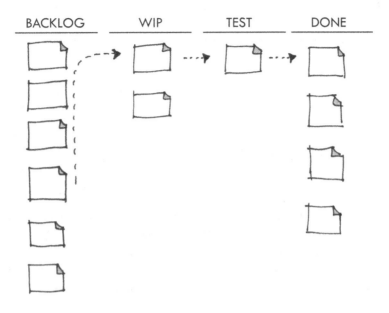

BACKLOG     WIP     TEST     DONE

setting a WIP limit of two. I found that working at more than two items at a time got me distracted. When a chapter was completed, I moved it to "Editing & Review" so that I could get external review and comments on it. And when the work was completed, I moved it to "Done".

I know of friends who have used Kanban boards to plan a variety of projects, including the renovation of their home, the organization of their wedding, or the distribution of chores among family members during a weekend.

## Build your Kanban board on a wall not on a digital tool

A Kanban board is useful to create an environment of collaboration and transparency, especially at the beginning of a new project or when the team comes together for the first time. My recommendation is to create a Kanban board on the wall and use stickies or User Story cards to represent the items as they move through the board. This allows everyone on the team to visualize the status of the work, and negotiate what to work on next.

Having the board on a wall that everyone can see at any time is a great way to visualize the work, create alignment across the team, and practice the use of the Kanban board. Once the mechanics are ingrained, and the team is comfortable with its process, you can digitize the contents and move to a digital tool like Jira or Trello to get added benefits like remote collaboration and automatic tracking of metrics.

FURTHER READING

..........................................................................................................

https://leankit.com/learn/kanban/kanban-board/

..........................................................................................................

https://en.wikipedia.org/wiki/Kanban_board

..........................................................................................................

# USER STORIES, EPICS, FEATURES

Throughout my career, I have worked in organizations that had clear boundaries between the technology and business departments and struggled to build a cohesive collaboration between them. This is often the case even in companies that have adopted Agile, as the reporting chain is built by functional area. But more than how people are functionally organized within the company, it's important how they collaborate and foster communication between functional boundaries.

## WHAT'S WRONG WITH REQUIREMENTS

When the technology department (the people doing the work) and the business department (the people deciding what needs to be done) act as two separate entities, the work is usually formalized with lengthy requirement documents that are handed from one department to the other. Requirements typically specify what a system should do, and how it should do it, in all possible details. They can be quite technical, and as such, may require some time to put together. To the tech team, requirements are like directives: there should be no interpretation and instead they should be implemented exactly as specified. This often results in a limited ability to adapt to changing market and customer conditions, subjectivity in interpretation of what a requirement really means, and a reduced opportunity to leverage the team's expertise to design a better solution for the customer.

### "I want a fast car"

To explain the importance of developing a common understanding of the requirements and closing the gap between the business and the development teams, I often do the following exercise with my teams or students in my classes.

Start by giving each person a blank sheet of paper and a pen or a marker. Then, ask them to draw a car based on their interpretation of the following requirement: "I want a fast car". Give them a few minutes and then ask them to share their drawings. Do the drawings show different types of cars, or did most people draw some version of a sports car?

Repeat the exercise, this time giving them some context about who the user is. For example: "As a grandma, I want a fast car". Have the drawings changed? Having a common understanding of the end user inevitably changes the interpretation of the requirement.

Finally, give them one more piece of information. This is the context, or the "why". What goal or purpose does the end user want to achieve? What if the requirement was: "As a grandma, I want a fast car, so that I can navigate the school parking lots easily and quickly".

This story is based on my mom. Of six grandchildren, two live nearby and she picks them up from school and takes them to after-school activities every day. The school grounds are always busy at dismissal time and getting in and out of the parking lot is hectic. She drives a small car to make it easier for her to navigate the maze of vehicles and fit into tight spots. In her context, a "fast" car is small, agile, and easy to get in and out of parking spots.

With shared information about the end user, their needs, and the benefits they expect to get from our work, we can develop a better understanding of the requirements and align the development team's understanding with the business and user needs. User Stories bring to life this shared understanding.

## User Stories focus on user value

A common format to write work items for a Backlog, a User Story can be used to describe a new feature, an enhancement to an existing capability, or a bug fix. User

Stories originated in the late '90s in an Agile method called XP Programming and have since been widely accepted among other Agile practices, including Scrum.

User Stories are very different from a list of requirements. User Stories focus on the value for the end users, rather than technical functionality of the system. Instead of directing how a feature should be implemented, User Stories describe what benefits the user should gain from that feature. Instead of forcing the development team to follow a list of directives, User Stories involve everyone in a conversation to define the best way to build a feature and deliver the intended benefits.[2]

User Stories are a great tool to foster cross-functional team collaboration and incorporate agility and customer-focus into the development process. They help by creating an environment where the technology and the business teams work together, breaking the inter-department barrier of the organization. Instead of writing lengthy requirement documents, User Stories contain just enough details to drive a conversation between technology and business, and remove barriers between the teams. Instead of writing all the technical requirements upfront, User Stories assume that the work is done just-in-time (JIT). Technical details, requirements, implementation, architecture, performance emerge over time and are negotiated among team members when they are ready and able to work on a specific feature.

## USER STORY FORMAT

A User Story always takes the point of view of the end user (that's why it's called a "User Story" :-)) and describes what actions the end user may do with it, and what benefits they may gain from it. The typical format of a User Story briefly explains the "who", the "what", and the "why":

"As a <type of user>, I want to <action to perform> so that <benefit I gain>"

- **Type of user:** Who is going to use that feature?

- **Goal or action:** What is the user doing with that feature?

- **Benefit I gain:** What value does the user gain or what problem does he or she need to solve?

A User Story is written on a card, rather than in a long requirements document. The card limits the space available for details, is easy to move, change, or throw away if needed, and allows everyone to have a shared understanding of the objectives of the work. User Stories provide just enough details to understand their goal and scope, but leave to the team to discuss and negotiate the requirements. Hence, User Stories are not intended to replace interactions but rather to foster conversations among all stakeholders (team members, customers, management, etc.). Any technical details

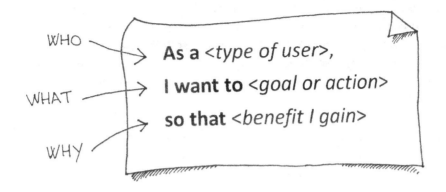

that are deemed essential for the testing and validation of the work are usually written on the back of the card and called "acceptance criteria".

## Who the user is

The "user" of a User Story should always be qualified and specific. Using just a generic description of "user" is not very useful because it doesn't tell you anything about who that user really is or what context the user operates in. The same goes for using a substitute for the word "user", like "customer".

When the "user" is properly qualified, it helps everyone understand the context of that user and make assumptions on his or her needs. A properly qualified "user" also helps everyone know whom the User Story delivers value to. If you have developed specific Personas, you can use these Personas in User Stories. Just make sure everyone on the team is aligned with the Persona's definition and needs.

For example, a "passenger in need of a ride home", a "truck driver", a "call center operator", or "Bob, the single father with a foreclosed home" are all better definitions of "user".

## TIPS

User Stories are placeholders for conversations. You can use the User Story format, or use your own format if it helps to make things easier. The point is, regardless of how well a User Story is written, it should never replace a conversation within the team.

> TRY
> THIS

Often, it's through team collaboration that we find better ways of doing things. Don't let the potential in your team go to waste — instead foster an environment where everyone is invited to participate, comment, and offer alternative points of view.

You will be amazed by how much a User Story may evolve, get richer in details, or be completely upended as the result of a productive conversation with the team. You may have all the requirements solidified, or they may still be very loose. Either way, use the User Story as a guideline to discuss what you intend to achieve, how it fits into the general vision of the product, and what specific tasks need to be done.

As a passenger in a taxi, I want to rate my driver so that others know about the comfort level of his or her car.

As a chef in a food truck, I want to know the weather forecast so that I may be able to estimate the number of customers for today.

As a single parent traveling with a small child, I want to research options for kid entertainment on a plane so that I may be able to sleep part of the flight.

As a developer on this team, I want to install an automatic testing engine so that I can deliver better code and fewer defects.

Examples of User Stories

## Sizing a User Story

Einstein told us that time is relative. My wife knows it very well, as my time estimates are always wrong ("you should double it, I know you will be late..." she would say). We also know that plans are subject to change as we learn more about a project while we are doing it. Estimates are usually done at the beginning of a project, and that's when we know the least about the actual work. When we do estimates based on time, we use a measure that is inherently vague, and create the false expectation of predictability.

So, when estimating a User Story, it's always better to do so by accounting for complexity, amount of work, uncertainty. In essence, we estimate based on the effort required to complete that User Story, and not based on time. There are a handful of methods commonly used to size User Stories, including t-shirt sizing and modified Fibonacci series. These methods give a rough estimate of the effort required to complete the Story.

- **T-Shirt sizing** assigns a relative size to each Story using any of the following "sizes": XS, S, M, L, XL.

- **Modified Fibonacci** is a series of numbers that can be assigned as Story Point to each Story to identify its size. The values are chosen from the series: 1, 2, 3, 5, 8, 13, 20, 40, 100 (modified Fibonacci series).

In either case the absolute size of a User Story is not important. What matters is the relative size compared to other Stories. Often, sizing a set of Stories starts from the smallest one, and then all others are sized relative to the first one.

## Big Stories make Epics and Features

### Epics

A very large User Story is often called an Epic. Epics usually span multiple development cycles or multiple releases, and require a considerable effort to complete. A development team never works on Epics as these are too big to fit within a Sprint or a development period. Instead, Epics are used by the product managers to identify high-level objectives for the business and negotiate priorities and roadmaps for large, important initiatives.

Once an Epic is prioritized, the product manager splits it into Features and User Stories, so that the development team can begin the work. Some of the Stories may be developed together, and others may be postponed. That means that an Epic may not be released at once, but it could be split in multiple releases. Once all the Stories belonging to an Epic are completed, then the Epic itself is completed.

### Features

Features are useful as they help to prioritize capabilities that users value or that the business wants, without the fine details of User Stories. By prioritizing Features, product managers can more easily visualize a roadmap, and share it with business stakeholders.

Features are larger than a User Story, but not as large as an Epic. Usually they span several development periods or Sprints, but are completed within a given release and their functionality is released all at once.

A Feature is usually split into multiple User Stories. The Stories are then worked together or in close proximity, so that the entire Feature can be released at once. As with larger Epics, a Feature is completed once all its Stories are completed.

## Getting a User Story done

The development team should begin working on a User Story only when all the details are properly defined, and external dependencies are sorted out. Starting the work on a User Story that is not "ready" for development and then stopping the work halfway because another team is late in providing what's needed is not an efficient use of development time. It's better to wait until the Story is "ready" and then do all the development work at once.

The definition of "ready" may vary from team to team depending on the particular work it is doing. For example, a web development team may consider a User Story as "ready" only when all the graphic assets have been provided by the design team, or when the product manager has received approval from other departments (e.g. Legal, Marketing, Security, Training) for all the contents to publish on the site.

"Ready" items may be prioritized and wait in the Backlog for their turn at development, but as soon as the team has an opening, they can be worked on.

Conversely, how do you know when the work on a User Story is completed? The developers and the product manager need to have a shared understanding of the conditions of satisfaction to consider a User Story as "done". These conditions are commonly documented with the Acceptance Criteria for each of the User Stories, and a shared Definition of Done.

### Acceptance Criteria

Acceptance Criteria are written on a User Story-by-User Story basis. They are conditions of satisfaction (aka testing requirements) to validate that the work on the User Story is completed. Since the Acceptance Criteria are written for each User Story, they are specific to that Story. For example, a login page on a website may list criteria that are very different from those listed for a page that allows a customer to pay with a credit card.

- The developer uses the Acceptance Criteria as requirements to validate their code and build unit/functional tests.

- A platform for automatic testing may use the Acceptance Criteria as a list of conditions to test the new work. ATDD (Automatic Test-Driven Development) employs this specifically, often in a particular format (e.g. Gherkin).

## Definition of "Done"

There are conditions of satisfaction that must be true for every User Story. For example, a team may require that every User Story encrypts the data a certain way, or that the code integrates within a given build. A bank may require that any work satisfies a minimum level of security, whereas a premium brand may require that any customer-facing material be approved by its Marketing department. The Definition of Done is a cross-functional checklist of all the activities the team must verify before completing each work item.

Instead of repeating these conditions in the Acceptance Criteria for every User Story, a team creates a Definition of Done that applies to every work item they complete. The criteria listed in the Definition of Done are common criteria that apply to all User Stories.

If you have multiple teams working at the same product, their Definitions of Done should be aligned to ensure that work is completed consistently across teams and can be properly integrated.

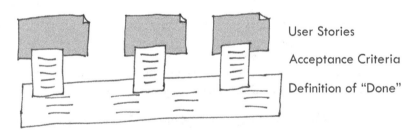

User Stories

Acceptance Criteria

Definition of "Done"

Acceptance Criteria versus Definition of "Done"

## FURTHER READING

Mike Cohn, *User Stories Applied: For Agile Software Development*, Addison-Wesley Signature Series

# PRIORITIZATION

In any project, there is usually more work to do than there is time or resources available. This is particularly true if you are using an Agile framework such as Scrum where the work in each iteration is limited in scope and time. When there are constraints, it's always useful to prioritize the work so that you can deliver the highest value first, to your customers and to your business.

You should prioritize your backlog as often as necessary. The prioritization activity is also an opportunity to revisit what is important for your customers, for your business, and for your stakeholders. Use this as an opportunity to collaborate and incorporate feedback.

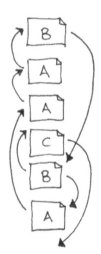

Perfect opportunities to re-prioritize your backlog:

- When a new idea, opportunity, or solution comes along

- When internal factors such as a change of strategy or constraints cause a re-alignment of priorities

- When external factors such as business environment, competition, or regulation affect some of the decisions you made earlier

- Before Sprint planning, before planning the next release, before a new PI planning session when using SAFe

There are many ways to prioritize your backlog, based on the project specifics, the time available, or the level of details you have.

## THE MOSCOW METHOD

The MoSCoW method (an acronym for Must, Should, Could, and Won't) is a simple put powerful tool to prioritize a list of items. It helps to collaborate with stakeholders and incorporate their feedback into the scheduling of a project.[3]

The method uses four buckets, and at the end of the process all the items must be placed in one of the buckets depending on the relative priority assigned to them.

**MUST**: Features that are deemed necessary to deliver the expected customer experience or the main benefits. These features are critical to the success of a product or are needed to validate your solution.

**SHOULD**: Features that are important, but not necessary to deliver the core experience of the product. They also may be critical but may not have a time constraint.

**COULD**: Just because we can build a feature it doesn't mean we should. In this bucket goes every feature that could improve the customer experience or deliver incremental value, if we have time to work on it.

**WON'T**: Everything else not deemed necessary or important goes in this bucket. This is often called the "WOULD LIKE TO" bucket. Items in this bucket are not discarded, they are just saved for a later time.

The MoSCoW method is simple and quick, and creates alignment within the team and the stakeholders. However, it does not allow for prioritization within each bucket, i.e. among all the features in the "MUST" bucket, which one should you do first?

........................................................................................................................

TRY
THIS

## TIP

Set a limit for the "MUST" bucket, to avoid putting all the work in it. For example, decide that only 25-30% of all features can be put in that bucket. This forces prioritization decisions.

## BUY-A-FEATURE

Buy-A-Feature is a great tool to source interest from your customers about a set of features and to understand how they make tradeoffs between them. It's effective at providing a high-level prioritization based on your customers' preferences, perceived value, and expectations. There are many versions of this tool, and many ways it can be used. Luke Hohmann provides a great description of it in the book "Innovation Games".[4]

It can be used to understand what customers value more in a set of competing features. This is the case when the business has a list of features, alternative options, or attributes of a product and wants to validate with customers which set of options is perceived as more valuable.

Buy-A-Feature can be employed as a relatively quick method to evaluate a large set of features with multiple people, in a limited time. Customers "buy" features that they would like in the next release using virtual money you give them.

## In-person, team-based format

This is useful when you can work with a group of end users or stakeholders together in the same room. In its simplest form, it's composed a few steps:

**Preparation:** Start with a list of features (that you have prepared upfront). Assign each feature a "price". This is a number that represents the development effort, time, or cost required to build that feature.

**Step 1:** Give each participant some $ (or Euro, or whatever currency you prefer): no more than one third of the total cost of all features. This is not real money, but a virtual currency. Think of it as Monopoly money.

**Step 2:** Ask your customers to buy as many, or as few, features as they like. They can spend the money on multiple features, or put all the money on one. They can also pull resources to buy features that would be too expensive for just one person.

**Step 3:** Once finished, identify the features that were purchased (those that received at least enough money to cover for their "price"), and those that were rejected.

## TIPS

TRY THIS

A few tips:

- Prices should vary so that not all the features have the same price.
- The total cost of all features should be higher than the money you give your customers, so that not all features can be purchased, forcing prioritization. As a ballpark, assume your users can only buy one-third to one-half of all features.
- You can force collaboration by having some features cost more than what a single user has to spend, so that customers need to pool their money together to buy them.
- Optimum group size is between four to eight to ensure collaboration. If you have more than 10 people, split them into two groups.
- The list of priorities you get tells you what customers value, not necessarily what you should build next. You may need to evaluate other decisions before proceeding to development.

## FURTHER READING

.........................................................................................................

For more info: http://www.innovationgames.com/buy-a-feature/

.........................................................................................................

## Online format

If you cannot get your users together in a room, you can create an alternate version of the tool using online surveys. Make a list of all features and add a box next to each feature to enter a point value. You can invite your users to invest their virtual money on as many or as few features, following similar rules as described earlier.

This is a quick way to get feedback on a large list of features from your stakeholders or customers, and can be useful in the early stages of planning. Be careful though because this method has several limitations:

• Since this is done online, you don't get direct feedback or the opportunity to discuss alternative solutions that your users may come up with

• There can be inherent bias depending on the description of each item, or the understanding by each of the participants

At Capital One we used this method to learn about priorities for a new tool we were planning. The end users where the bankers in our retail locations, so we invited a few of them to provide their input. We also invited some of their executive management.

A REAL STORY

We built the Buy-a-Feature tool using an online survey system, and then asked everyone to indicate how much money they'd be willing to spend for each of the features, up to a maximum of $100 total.

We had purposely divided them in two different groups of people as we expected their input to be different. In fact, the preferences they expressed for the features they wanted in the new tool were pretty much in competition between the two groups. Bankers wanted features that made their job easier and helped them serve the customers better. The management wanted features to streamline processes and improve efficiencies.

We discarded those features that had not received many investments, and instead focused on those that had been selected by either group. We then checked each feature for feasibility and effort, and ranked them. Some features had received a substantial high approval by the users, but also required a very large effort to build.

We decided to focus on those features that had received a high approval and required relatively small effort to build (high Value-over-Effort ranking). These made our MVP list. The rest was prioritized for future releases.

## VALUE-OVER-EFFORT

Sometimes you may have work items that are comparable in terms of value but vary considerably in terms of effort required to build them. Which one should you start first? Value-over-Effort is a quick method to understand the relative relationship between value and effort, to help prioritize your work and deliver value faster (its more complex cousin, WSJF, is discussed later). This method can be used alone, or in partnership with others. For example, it could be used to prioritize the "MUST" bucket of a MoSCoW prioritization. Its premise is to deliver the highest value items first. By calculating Value-over-Effort, you are considering the highest value items in comparison to the time it takes to build them.

$$PRIORITY = \frac{VALUE}{EFFORT}$$

To estimate VALUE and EFFORT for each item, use the sizing methods for User Stories, such as the modified Fibonacci series (1, 2, 3, 5, 8, 13, 20, 40, 100).

**VALUE** represents the relative value each feature delivers to the customers and to the business.

**EFFORT** is an estimate of the amount of work it takes to build a feature. It's usually estimated in terms of total effort (amount of work, complexity, unknowns, etc.) rather than time, as the estimate of time is usually tricky (individual perceptions of time vary, work is never done in isolation, and time cannot be easily measured, etc.).

The chart below shows how proper prioritization helps to deliver value faster. Even if the total time to build all four features is the same, by changing the priorities we can affect how quickly we deliver value.

| Item | Value | Effort (Time) |
| --- | --- | --- |
| A | 1 | 4 |
| B | 1 | 1 |
| C | 2 | 4 |
| D | 2 | 1 |

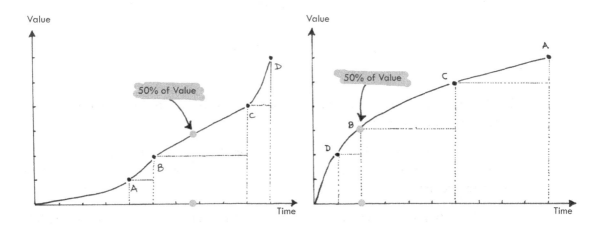

Prioritization allows to delivering value faster

The chart on the left shows the value generated by following the list as is. Notice that to reach 50% of the total value, you need to wait for about seven periods.

The chart on the right shows the value generated if the items were prioritized using Value-over-Effort. To deliver 50% of total value, it only takes two periods (or less than 1/3 of the time).

The Value-over-Effort method is a simplified version of WSJF and can be used for a quick estimation of a list of items. The next section is dedicated to WSJF.

# WEIGHTED SHORTEST JOB FIRST (WSJF)

The Weighted Shortest Job First (or WSJF) is a prioritization technique that calculates the value for each of the work items expressed as "Cost of Delay" and weighs it against the effort it would take to build the item, called "Duration". The goal is to identify the items that can deliver the highest value in the shortest time.

In its simplest form, WSJF is defined as the Cost of Delay divided by Duration. However, the Cost of Delay includes several components, and each one should be analyzed individually: "Value", "Value reduction over time", and "Risk of delay".

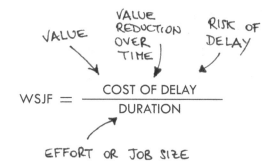

The three components of Cost of Delay in the numerator are evaluated feature by feature in numerical values:

**Value**: It represents both the value delivered to the customers and the value generated to the business (in general, for a healthy business these two should not be in contradiction :-))

**Value reduction over time** (also called **Time criticality**): It specifies if the feature has a time-sensitivity because its value decreases over time, or because by waiting too long it may lose its effectiveness.

**Risk of delay**: It quantifies the level of risk that waiting to build that feature may expose the business to. For example, an upcoming change in regulation may require you to change a feature in your product by a specific deadline, and failure to doing so may result in hefty fines. Or, a competitor may exploit a technological breakthrough and if you wait to do the same you risk losing market share.

In WSJF, a backlog item is called a "job". The **Duration** is an estimate of the effort it would take to complete the job; hence it is also called Job Size. Because usually items are written in User Story format, the estimate of effort can be done using standard sizing techniques, such as the modified Fibonacci series (1, 2, 3, 5, 8, 13, 20, 40, 100).

This has the advantage of not only being a familiar sizing technique, but also to be already in numerical format, allowing a quick use of the formula.

To calculate WSJF follow the procedure:

Step 1. Start with "Value".

Step 2. Identify the item in your backlog that has the lowest Value. Assign this item a Value of 1, as this becomes your baseline for the column Value.

Step 3. For all the other items, evaluate their Value in comparison to the baseline identified in step 2. Assign each item a Value using the modified Fibonacci scale.

Step 4. Once you have completed the entire column, repeat the process for the second column "Value reduction over time" and then for the column "Risk of delay". Identify the baseline item in each column and estimate all items in comparison to the baseline.

Step 5. Finally, repeat the process for the column "Duration", starting with the item with the smallest effort, and then move on to all other items.

Step 7. Calculate WSJF for each item: add up Value + Value reduction over time + Risk of delay, and divide by Duration. This is the WSJF score for each of the items.

Step 8. Sort the items based on their WSJF score. The highest score indicates the highest priority.

## Try this exercise: Planning vacation activities

WSJF is a useful prioritization technique, but it may feel a bit overwhelming at first. To get familiar with it in a fun setting, you can do the following exercise.[5] This works well either alone or together with your team.

TRY
THIS

Imagine being on vacation on a Caribbean island. Together with your family, friends, or significant other, you are guests of a premium resort. There are only two days left in your vacation, and then you will return home. You want to make sure to spend these last two days wisely, enjoy your time there, and create memories that you can take back home.

After reading the list of possible activities given to you by the resort, you realize you may only have time to do two of these activities… which ones to choose? You need to prioritize the list and choose the activities that not only are most enjoyable but also create the greatest memories. Some activities have a time criticality: they are in high demand, and if you don't reserve your spot now, you won't be able to do them.

Work your way through the table, estimating all activities one column at a time. Once you have filled all columns, calculate WSJF. The highest number indicates the activity you should select to maximize the time remaining on the island. Now, relax and enjoy your vacation!

| WORKSHEET **VACATION ACTIVITIES** | VALUE<br><br>Having fun, meeting other people, getting fit | TIME CRITICALITY<br><br>Limited availability, high demand (get it now, or lose it) | BEST MEMORIES<br><br>Maximize opportunity to bring back memories | TOTAL<br><br>Also called: Cost of Delay | JOB SIZE<br><br>Amount of time to commit or $$$ | WSJF<br><br>What's the highest priority? |
|---|---|---|---|---|---|---|
| *Happy hour pool-side* | | | | | | |
| *"Swimming with dolphins" boat cruise* | | | | | | |
| *Bocce ball tournament* | | | | | | |
| *Tennis match with Roger Federer* | | | | | | |
| *Little Princess contest for girls* | | | | | | |
| *Horse riding tour of island* | | | | | | |
| *Sailing cruise at sunset* | | | | | | |

1. Start with the Value column: find the activity with the lowest value and give it a 1. This is your baseline for the column.
2. Estimate Value for all the other activities, relative to the baseline you selected.
3. Complete one column at a time, repeating the process for each of the columns.

To estimate, use the Story Point values: 1 2 3 5 8 13 20 40 100

Add up Value, Time Criticality, and Risk Reduction for each activity

Divide Cost of Delay by Job Size and get the WSJF value for each activity

You can download the exercise worksheet from:

https://www.5dvision.com/docs/wsjf/

## Keeping track of the numbers

There are many ways to keep track of these calculations. You can use an Excel table that lists all the Features/Stories and provides a column for each component in WSJF and the resulting priority.

Alternatively, you can write a Feature/User Story on a card, and jot the number for each component, including the WSJF score on the card itself. This is a visual medium that allows for collaboration and is easier to share with your team.

You can download the template of a Feature/User Story card:

https://www.5dvision.com/docs/user-story-card/

**Title**

*As an online shopper, I want to search for books and filter based on my interests so that I buy a book that I like to read*

**Epic/Feature**

*Custom search with filters*

| Value | | | Effort | Priority |
|---|---|---|---|---|
| *13* | *2* | *8* | *13* | *1.77* |

A User Story card, with WSJF prioritization

## FURTHER READING

http://www.scaledagileframework.com/wsjf/

https://en.wikipedia.org/wiki/Shortest_job_next

# KEEPING TECHNICAL DEBT IN CHECK

Product development activities are hectic, as teams try to jam as many features as possible into a single release, and as the business pushes for higher productivity. At times, development teams make shortcuts as they push for a deadline; make architectural choices to fit into the current environment and delay updates to a later time; or delay fixing small problems as they push for bigger features to become available.

There is a silent enemy, it's the technical debt. And if it goes unchecked, over the long run it can wreak havoc in your product. Technical debt is an expression of cost, that is the cost to make changes, either because you need to fix things or because the product is too complex. The key to technical debt reduction is in working on it early and often, so to keep its cost low. The smaller the debt, the less difficult it is to fix it. By waiting and delaying, technical debt can only increase, making it harder to solve later.

Many consider technical debt as the number one cause of product failures over the long run. When an architecture becomes too rigid and too complex to upgrade, it cannot sustain the rhythm of innovation, and risks giving ground to competitive products. This is what happened to the Netscape browser, once the leading browser for the World Wide Web. But when Internet Explorer came along, Netscape could not easily adapt to the new competitive environment. Netscape lost market share until completely disappearing.

Depending on circumstances, technical debt can arise at any time, during the initial development, maintenance (fixing issues), or enhancements (building new capabilities). The key is to control technical debt to avoid the long-term problems it creates. Teams employ different techniques to manage technical debt, including:

## Reserve capacity

Reserve capacity for technical debt work. For example, a team may decide to reserve 15% of its time (or velocity) to work on technical debt. This approach requires a compromise with prioritization of new features. As the team receives pressure to work on new features, keeping technical debt work prioritized high enough can be difficult. Reserving capacity for technical debt reduction creates alignment on the entire team (development team together with product management and business) and transparency of what gets done.

## IP Sprint

Avoiding technical debt depends also on having the right development and testing infrastructure available to your team and using the latest technologies and tools available in the market. Teams need time to improve their infrastructure and learn new technologies. During an IP Sprint (Innovation and Planning) no new features get built. The "Innovation" part is dedicated to research (e.g. learning a new technology) and productivity enhancements (e.g. installing a new testing tool). The "Planning" part is dedicated to preparing the backlog for the next set of development Sprints and developing a shared understanding of what's coming next.

IP Sprints are a great way to build time for teams to improve how they do the work. Depending on the frequency at which they are done, IP Sprints can eat up quite a percentage of time, though. Striking a good balance between regular development Sprints and IP Sprint cadence is therefore a choice every organization needs to make. I found it useful to have an IP Sprint every four to six development Sprints.

## AUTOMATED TESTING AND CI/CD

As your application becomes increasingly complex, so is the task of testing every new functionality. Not only do you need to verify that the latest feature you built works, but also that everything else is still working fine. Without proper testing procedures, you risk that a recent change to the code impacts a feature that was built months ago. Unit testing is not enough as it is limited to the latest developments. To ensure quality and minimize technical debt, you need regression testing and automated testing.

### TIP

Make sure your team reserves time for implementing automation, installing the proper tools, and removing technical debt. It is good practice to add these activities to the Backlog and prioritize them as needed. An IP Sprint (Innovation and Planning Sprint) is also a good opportunity to dedicate focused time to these activities.

TRY
THIS

### Regression testing

Regression testing is a type of testing that verifies that software previously developed and tested still performs correctly even after it was changed by a recent development.[6] Changes may include new features, new libraries, software patches, OS and API upgrades, configuration changes. Any of these changes has the potential to affect any of the functionalities of your application. Often, the most difficult issues to catch are those created by changes in areas of the application not directly affected by those changes.

The goal of regression testing is to verify that any recent change has not introduced new problems. It's very unfortunate to see potentially great apps ruin their customer experience when a new feature is released and suddenly something else in another part of the app stops working. No matter the tool you use, regression testing should always be part of your toolkit.

Ever since BookingBug implemented regression testing, it runs more than 1,000 tests on every build. This allows the company to maintain the quality of its product and keep technical debt in check.

Regression testing is, however, not a magic wand. It can save a huge number of work hours and headaches, but it works its magic only when properly implemented. As most things in life, it is up to you to make good use of it.

Running regression testing manually can be a huge endeavor, especially in large or complex applications. For this reason, automatic testing tools are often used to simplify and speed up the regression testing of an application.

## FURTHER READING

https://en.wikipedia.org/wiki/Regression_testing

## Automated testing

Most testing procedures, including regression testing, can be laborious and time-consuming. In Agile environments where the development cycles are very short and resources are scarce, manual testing is usually limited to unit testing. Automated testing is becoming increasingly important for software projects of all sizes to automatically verify key functionality, conduct regression, and help teams deliver a great user experience at all times.

Automated testing tools offer to speed-up testing procedures, and to make them more effective. Whereas performing manual regression testing on a full application is not usually a feasible option, automated testing can do this with ease and speed. With automated testing we can perform a broader set of tests, at a deeper level, than what would be possible with manual techniques.

There are many tools for test automation. Depending on the type of app you build

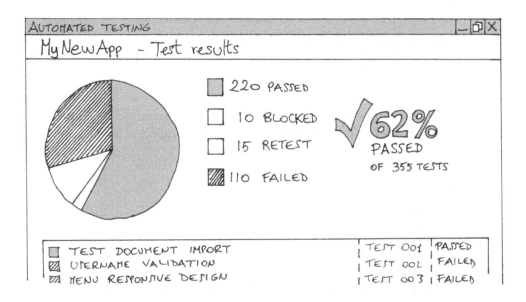

(web, mobile, stand-alone, custom) and your organization's preferences, you may find a suite of testing tools that fits your needs. A Google search offers many ways to discover and compare testing tools, for almost all possible needs.

## FURTHER READING

Learn more about different tools:
http://www.testingtools.com/test-automation

## Acceptance Test Driven Development (ATDD)

Acceptance Test Driven Development or ATDD is a technique used to bring the customer's point-of-view into the testing phase, before development is even started. Test cases are written in a human-friendly format that represents the expected outcome, benefit, or behavior of the test. The format can also be interpreted by a machine, and hence becomes automated.

The key benefit of ATDD is that it incorporates the customer experience into the design of the tests. It also expects a close collaboration between the members of the team in writing acceptance tests and describe how the system should work.

## FURTHER READING

Wikipedia: "Acceptance test–driven development"
https://en.wikipedia.org/wiki/Acceptance_test-driven_development

Acceptance Criteria can be written in a format that allows for automatic testing. One such format is defined by Gherkin, which is a language supported by the automated testing tool Cucumber. Gherkin uses the format:

Given <some preconditions>

When <some user action>

Then <testable result>

The use of Gherkin provides not only a machine-readable format for automatic testing, but also a business-friendly documentation that's easily readable by humans.

## FURTHER READING

https://github.com/cucumber/cucumber/wiki/Gherkin

https://en.wikipedia.org/wiki/Cucumber_(software)

https://cucumber.io/

## Continuous Integration/Continuous Delivery

Continuous Integration (CI) is the process employed by developers who check-in their code at frequent intervals and trigger an integration of the project. By doing this frequently, developers greatly reduce the risk that a late change may have a big impact on the project.

Continuous Delivery (CD) is designed to automate the delivery process, so that software can be released at any time. Companies that employ a Continuous Delivery methodology release new features on a daily basis, sometimes even multiple times a day.

The goal of Continuous Integration/Continuous Delivery is to build, test, integrate, and deploy software faster and more frequently, reducing the risks, costs, and time required for integration and deployment of larger increments.

One tool that has surged to fame is Jenkins, an open source tool available for many platforms and that was spun-off from an original project at Oracle. Jenkins is a continuous integration platform. It is also an automation server that can do much more with expansion plugins to the most common automated testing tools. Jenkins supports unit testing, automated testing, and regression testing.

## FURTHER READING

https://jenkins.io

https://www.tutorialspoint.com/jenkins/index.htm

Jez Humble, David Farley, *Continuous Delivery: Reliable Software Releases through Build, Test, and Deployment Automation*, Addison-Wesley, 2011

Kent Beck, *Test Driven Development: By Example*, Addison-Wesley, 2003

Gundecha Unmesh, *Selenium Testing Tools Cookbook*, Packt Publishing, 2012

George Ukkuru, *Test Automation best practices*, Kindle Edition, 2014

Lou Pedron, *Software Test Automation: Getting Started Guide for QA Managers, Quality Engineers and Project Managers*, Kindle Edition, 2015-2016

# BOOKINGBUG

BookingBug (www.bookingbug.com) is a company that provides scheduling and appointment-setting capabilities across a variety of industries. Founded in 2008 in the UK, in recent years it has built a strong reputation among enterprise customers around the world for its powerful platform and the breadth of customizations it offers. It is used by hundreds of organizations from banks to retailers and governments including Lego, Cisco, John Lewis, and the UK Government.[7, 8, 9] It was listed by the Financial Times in the "Future 100 UK" list in recognition of its growth and wider impact on its industry.[10]

Yet, it didn't start this way. In fact, it had a bumpy journey and along the way it risked losing a critical contract with a large US bank — the type of event that would have harmed its reputation and its hopes of international expansion.

This story is an excerpt from an interview with Glenn Shoosmith, Founder and CEO of BookingBug, who tells a story of humble beginnings, hard work, and near-death growth problems.[11]

It all started out of frustration with booking a local squash court. At the time, no sport center offered an online booking service, and he had to call to make a reservation, and then visit them in person to pay, in advance. Glenn soon realized that there was an opportunity to make things better, and that could potentially be a massive market. "Internet was very good at selling you goods, but was very bad at selling you services, beyond restaurants and hotels," said Glenn.

BookingBug spent its first few years building a platform for SMBs (Small-Medium Businesses). Initial customers included hair dressers, beauty salons, sport centers, and wedding photographers. This extreme variety of customers resulted in a product that was complex and yet hugely powerful, as it supported different payment systems, ecommerce systems, accounting systems, services, classes, courses, and events. Every customer had different needs, and BookingBug tried to solve every different problem by adding new features for each need.

The product suffered from massive feature creep. "What I did was go to a market segment, be not very effective at selling to them, and then add another feature for a different market segment and keep moving to the next segment, hoping that one would just magically sell," said Glenn. "Instead, what we should have done was take one market segment and work very hard on how to sell a beautiful product in that segment."

The first break came when Levi's in the UK found it through an online search on Google. They wanted a system to book an in-store appointment for a jeans-fitting campaign. They liked that BookingBug could be branded and skinned to match Levi's brand, and was able to support a lot of different features. "That was really our first 'enterprise' customer. And I realized that if I could sell it to 250 Levi's stores at once, this was far better than selling to 250 individual small businesses."

The pivotal moment was when John Lewis, the iconic department store in the UK, issued a tender offer for an appointment scheduling system for its website. BookingBug participated along with big service integrator names like Salesforce, Oracle, and the like. These were large companies, who employed thousands and could dedicate resources to this project. BookingBug had barely twelve employees and was managing several small business customers at a time.

John Lewis was the best brand name in department stores and had a strong reputation on customer service. An iconic company, they evaluated the bidders on various criteria, including how well they fit with John Lewis's brand and values. Going against the big guns in the IT industry was not easy. In a particular conversation, they asked about the number of UX experts available on the project. The big companies said they could put a thousand developers from India and they could all work on this project.

"We said, we got one. His name is Luke. And he is really good at building booking journeys. It's all he does; he builds booking journeys."

John Lewis liked that BookingBug had accumulated an expertise in appointment scheduling by working with many different small businesses in a variety of industries. In particular, it had expertise in managing beauty appointments. "We knew more about the business. We had a whole conversation about beauty, and of course we had hair dressers and we were able to talk about the complexity of beauty appointments and the scheduling rules, and the dynamics, things that these business people had not even thought about. We were able to convince them that we knew more than they did about their own business problems." This was the sort of expertise that the other IT companies could gain only by spending a ton of money in consulting fees.

BookingBug won the business. "It has been fantastic, but we put everything we had to deliver that solution. We worked 24/7, weekends and nights and overtime to make sure it worked. We promised a lot, we promised a few things we couldn't quite do, we had to work harder to actually then do it. We knew that if we got that right, and it was successful, the reputational shift for us would just be titanic."

And shortly thereafter other department stores started knocking at its doors. "As the dominos fall quite quickly you move from being the complete outsider no one is using, to suddenly the de facto solution that every department store wants." Even Harrods's knocked at its door.

Winning John Lewis allowed BookingBug to shift its focus away from SMB and instead dedicate resources to large customers. Soon, it had a few other enterprise customers including some in the US, a major market that represented the next opportunity for expansion. At this point, scalability became a big issue. Suddenly it had multiple projects open at the same time. Working with large customers required a lot more focus, support, and customization work. Even as the company started bringing in more people, it was hard to balance everything it wanted to do.

This was the classic problem startups go through when their market grows, and they need to refresh their technology. Suddenly, they have been in business a few years, and new customers are coming in. The system they built starts feeling old, and they start building a new system that looks shiny but does not have all the features of the old one. With limited resources, they try to do both things at the same time, and they end up doing both badly.

"People don't like the old system because it looks dated, they want the new system, then they try it, but they complain it's buggy. And you are trying to support both systems at the same time and you are trying to finish the new system while delivering to clients. This was the real struggle we had in 2015-16."

At this point Capital One, a large US bank, invited BookingBug to implement an appointment system for their branches. Capital One represented for BookingBug a pivotal opportunity to grow the US market and build a reputation in the banking industry, traditionally hard to win. But it had not worked with banks before and it was not ready for the hard requirements they imposed.

The product suffered from too much accumulated technical debt. It made it hard to customize things, and caused all sorts of problems. Because the company had no regression testing in place, as it built new features for the bank, other things started breaking up. It also had no documentation ready, so the development teams within the bank had a very hard time integrating with the BookingBug's API.

"Because when you do a startup, you are hacking a product together and you got no money and you are fine to ship it to small businesses, you don't care about testing, so you don't test. You are delivering features very, very quickly. Everything is rapidly developed and shipped. The big shift we had to go through, as we shifted to selling to enterprises, in particular, to selling to banks, was that we had to suddenly say 'I need to QA things', 'I need continuous integration', all those things that I had left behind and now are back. If you break things, banks will not forget that. You can anger a few SMBs and live with it, but if you anger a few banks your reputation tanks."

It got so bad that Capital One threatened to quit the contract. That's when Glenn got on a plane and flew to the US to present how he was going to fix things and deliver on the BookingBug promise.

"We had to really focus on improving the quality, improving the customer service, improving the customer relationship, and really what we did was that we actually stopped selling," recalled Glenn.

"I told my sales team: forget the next client. If we don't successfully deliver the clients we already sold to, there is not going to be a next set of clients. Because if you sell the next one, how are we going to deliver to those we have already? If we are not going to deliver to Capital One, we are never going to have references. If Capital One cancels, that completely stops the business. We basically cut down on product development. We just focused on quality and on delivery. This was the only way we could save the business and get our reputation back on course."

Glenn and his team spent most of the next year paying off technical debt and fixing legacy issues with the product, upgrading all sorts of bits in the system that were fragile or broken. Glenn himself joined the development team to provide guidance and add an additional resource. For some time, it was all hands on deck. The team built a test suite with full regression testing and thousands of tests in place. It adopted Agile practices, implementing Scrum, test-driven development, and continuous integration. All these efforts paid off enormously in terms of communication (both internally and with external customers) and in terms of quality at delivery.

"We had a lot of growing up as a company. I think what Capital One needed to see was strong leadership from our side. And then we obviously had to back it up with delivery. I think we were able to reset the relationship and give confidence back to Capital One. We were having a few growth and teething problems, but we were worth sticking with. It's difficult when you don't see someone in the eyes, you think it's just another vendor. But when I showed up and I said no, this is my business, this is my life, this is hugely important, it created the connection, a bit more trust. Hopefully that paid off well."

"Many people don't realize how many years of grinding hard work it takes to really grow a business. People think that starting your business and being an entrepreneur means having time to relax and go to the beach. But that's not true. Being an entrepreneur and building a business is hard work. I lead by example, and if I ask my team to work hard, I work even harder."

# REFERENCES

1.  For more information on Panda updates, see: "History of Google Algorithm Updates", https://www.searchenginejournal.com/google-algorithm-history/ or "Confirmed: A Panda Refresh, Version #23", https://www.seroundtable.com/google-update-maybe-16121.html

2.  Alistair Cockburn "A story card is a promise for a conversation" - http://alistair.cockburn.us/Origin+of+user+story+is+a+promise+for+a+conversation

3.  Source: Wikipedia https://en.wikipedia.org/wiki/MoSCoW_method

4.  Luke Hohmann, *Innovation Games*, Addison-Wesley 2007

5.  Courtesy of Hard Yards, LLC - https://www.hardyards.com

6.  Source: Wikipedia: https://en.wikipedia.org/wiki/Regression_testing

7.  List of customers https://www.bookingbug.com/customers

8.  "Creating profitable engagements for retail banks" https://www.bookingbug.com/financial-services

9.  "Customer stories" https://www.bookingbug.com/customers

10. Financial Times, "Future 100 UK" - https://ig.ft.com/future-100/2018/

11. From an interview with Glenn Shoosmith, February 17, 2017

# NOTES

The plan for a Minimum Viable Product becomes visible when using Product Journey Maps

# [ 10 ]

## DEPLOY

Building a product is hard work. Executing all the right steps through Discovery, Design, and Development, and finally having a tangible product that is ready for launch requires a lot of energy and commitment. When the hard work finally comes together, the Deployment phase is exciting — your product is ready to see the light for the first time. That champagne bottle you stored in the fridge can finally bring a moment of celebration to your team.

Sometimes, this is also the time when you discover that you are not ready. While the product you worked so hard to make is completed, other aspects of your commercialization strategy are lagging behind. These could be a marketing campaign, the expected support from your partners, training materials, or any other thing you need to properly support your product in the market. As you get closer to the launch date, some pieces may not come together as expected, and you must rush to get them ready.

As a business advisor in a startup incubator near Washington, DC, I've seen a recurring theme among new product launches. New startup founders identify a need in the market and build a cool, new app. They get it all done, with a fancy UI and plenty of interesting features. As soon as they launch it, they ask for help with marketing, because they see no traction in the market. Often, the marketing strategy is an afterthought. So is a clear understanding of the target customer segment. At this point, the company loses momentum, as it needs to go back to the drawing board and figure out the missing pieces.

Deployment should be an integral phase of the product development strategy. It's an important step in the 5D Vision of product development. Ideally, organizations and teams should consider how they are going to launch a new product while they are doing Discovery, Design, and Development. Ideas and opportunities in these early phases help in identifying the key components needed for Deployment (e.g. your initial target segment) and avoid waiting until the last minute to define your launch strategy.

# WHAT IS DEPLOYMENT?

To deploy a product means to launch it in the marketplace and make it available to its users. This phase is also called "commercialization", "launch", or "moving to production". Deployment is different from Delivery (the next phase) in that it focuses on launching a product in the marketplace, while Delivery focuses on measuring customer success.

The purpose of Deployment is to make your new product available in the marketplace. The new product could be an MVP (Minimum Viable Product), an incremental update, or a full-fledged new release. In any case, bringing it to market so that your end users can interact with it and possibly provide feedback, is a necessary step to validate the success of your idea.

Deployment is often a carefully orchestrated number of steps that need to happen in order and must be aligned across multiple teams. This is not only the responsibility of your IT Operations department, but rather of a cross-functional team with members from Marketing, Training, Support, and other departments which may be needed to fully support the launch of the new product.

## IT'S NOT ABOUT THE ROCKET

Deploying a product in the marketplace is never the end point but is always the beginning of a journey.

I like the analogy of deploying a rocket into space (think SpaceX): 3-2-1-FIRE! And your rocket lifts off. A successful launch is a huge moment of celebration and the conclusion of months of hard work and preparation for this single moment. But having the rocket lift off is not the end, it's just the beginning of a mission. You still must run the mission, manage the flight in space, dock at the Space Station, manage re-entry, collect telemetry data, and ensure the survival of the crew (if there is one onboard).

The same goes for your product. After you launch it, you need to market it, sell it, support it. You will have to collect feedback from your users, validate whether it satisfies their needs, and plan for future updates.

## Make sure your ecosystem is ready for launch

Iridium, a Motorola spinoff company that created a cellphone network using low-orbit satellites that could cover the entire planet, launched its product with great fanfare after 11 years of development. It ran a huge marketing push with full-page color ads in newspapers worldwide. And it was announced as a technological wonder for those business people in need of cellphone connection while traveling, or for those in regions poorly serviced by mobile phones.

Yet, when it launched, and for several months afterwards, there were no devices available. Motorola had partnered with other manufacturers to build and commercialize Iridium satellite phones, but the partners were not ready for launch. A couple of phones that Motorola had developed — mainly to demonstrate the service — were too bulky and had a limited battery life so that customers did not find them attractive. This, and other reasons, caused a quick demise of Iridium, going into bankruptcy less than two years after launch (see the Iridium story later in this chapter).

This is a classic example of a product launch that was not properly coordinated across all the parties in the ecosystem. Part of the Deployment preparedness activities is to make sure all supporting elements of the product's ecosystem are ready at launch — including partners, supply, distribution, marketing, training materials, customer support, etc.

## Know who your customers are

When Segway announced its product, it was touted as a technological wonder that would revolutionize transportation in cities. The company had planned to sell it to city residents who preferred the Segway to cars or public transportation for short commutes within the city. Yet, no customer saw it that way. The product was bulky and needed to be charged. It could carry only one person at a time, and had costs similar to a small utility car — which, instead, could accommodate multiple passengers or other things. City residents didn't buy it. Segway had targeted the wrong user segment.

Without knowing who your target customers are, it's very difficult — or very expensive — to market your product and create traction. In his book "Crossing the

Chasm", author Geoffrey Moore talks about the Early Adopters.[1] This is a key customer segment that experiences a strong need and is willing to adopt your product early on. Even if they have to put up with some deficiencies with your product, they have the personal interest to try it out and believe the benefits they get from it outweigh the cons. Knowing who your Early Adopters are is, therefore, a key component of any successful market launch.

### FURTHER READING

Geoffrey A. Moore, *Crossing the Chasm: Marketing and Selling High-Tech Products to Mainstream Customers*, Harper Collins, 2006

## It's about the full customer experience

Customers buy an experience, not a bundle of features. They don't buy a cell phone just to have a glass-covered plastic device in their pocket. They buy it because it allows them to communicate with their friends and family, to discover what goes on around them, to get navigation assistance, to enjoy a perceived status symbol, and possibly several other reasons.

Customers care about the overall experience they get from your product and the perceived value they receive from it. How are the customers going to learn about your product? How are they going to buy it? How are they going to incorporate it in

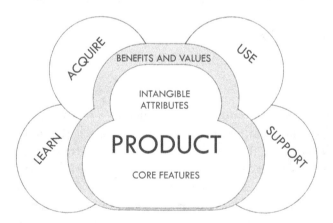

their daily lives? The answers to these questions go beyond just a set of features that the product offers and explore the full customer experience that your end users really care about. This includes acquisition, packaging, marketing, support, training.

You can think of it as a sort of Russian doll. In the center is your product, with its core set of features; next to the core features are the intangible properties of your product and its emotional appeal (e.g. brand recognition, status symbol, environmental friendliness, etc.) that customers may appreciate and value. Each feature provides a benefit and delivers value to the customer, so on the second ring we place benefits and values. Then on the outer layer we have four areas needed to deliver the full customer experience:

## LEARN

How are customers going to learn about it? For example marketing and advertising activities, promotions, social networking.

## ACQUIRE

How are they going to acquire it? This includes the purchase experience, online versus in-store, distribution, packaging.

## USE

How are they going to use it? Do they use the way it was designed and intended for, or do they invent new uses for it? How often do they use it? Do they incorporate the product into their daily lives, or do they use it only sporadically?

## SUPPORT

How do they learn how to use it and get support if they get stuck? This may include training manuals, online support, customer service.

The idea is that by working through each of these areas and solidifying your understanding of the activities taking place at each stage, you can provide a better customer experience and therefore a better product. Ideally you would plan how to tackle these areas in the early stages of product development.

## THE FIVE Ws OF DEPLOYMENT

Consider answering the following questions to start thinking about how you are going to Deploy your next product: Who, What, Where, When, and Why.

### WHO

Whom do you launch to?

Consider the target segment(s) and create a clear description of your users. You can refer to the Problem Statement, Personas, and 5D Canvas you worked on during Discovery for insights on needs, challenges, and opportunities with your target users.

Facebook famously started with college students and opened its service to everyone only after it had already acquired most colleges in the US.

### WHAT

What are you going to deploy?

Think about not only your core product, but also additional components to enhance the user experience. Is this a new product, or an incremental release? Do your customers need support, training, installation assistance?

Thumbtack, an online marketplace for local services, launched in 2009 its online web service. The information about the business providers is user generated. However, the founders realized early on that if they wanted to appeal to new prospective customers, they needed to have an initial list of local businesses from day one. So, they worked on the supply side first, scraping content from multiple sources and filling up their database with information about local providers.[2]

### WHERE

Where are you going to launch?

For example, many companies start small then expand. Uber launched its MVP in San Francisco and perfected its offering before expanding to other cities, and is doing so one city at a time.

## WHEN

When are you going to launch?

Consider when it's best to launch. Is there a seasonality in your market? Is there time pressure from another competitor or from customer expectations? Is there a time where users are more likely in need of your offering?

For example, some successful movie franchises are always launched around the same time of the year. The six original Star Wars movies were all released in May.[3] New Apple devices are traditionally announced at the end of Summer.

## WHY

Why should your customers care?

Having a compelling value proposition and communicating it to customers is essential to make sure they understand your product's benefits. Your customers are going to invest in your product — their money, their time, their emotions — and you should help them understand why they should do it.

Explaining the "why" is probably the most important component of your launch strategy. This message should permeate your brand, your marketing, and any communication with your customers.

# IRIDIUM, THE EXCITEMENT AND A DEPLOYMENT FIASCO

Iridium launched its satellite mobile phone service in November 1998. It was a technological wonder, and promised communication coverage to the entire planet, including deserts, oceans, and poles. It was touted as the service that would revolutionize personal communications, at a time when terrestrial cellphone networks were still struggling to attract subscribers and define a common standard for interoperability. With a single Iridium phone, you could travel anywhere in the world and be connected at all times.

It had taken 11 years to build the system. Yet, not even a year after the service finally became available to the public, Iridium filed for bankruptcy. Its launch had been a failure, and the company had not been able to correct its course. It had failed to attract the subscriber base it was hoping for and was haunted by several other misguided actions. At the time, Iridium became the largest bankruptcy in US history.[4]

The Iridium story is fascinating for its technological wonder and rapid demise. It's also a story I'm personally connected to having worked for the European branch of Iridium just around the time when the company prepared to launch. The company I co-founded, Novaera Information Systems, built the entire web infrastructure for Iridium Italia, a joint venture between Iridium, Telespazio, and Telecom Italia that was responsible for the commercialization of the Iridium service across Europe. The original website is still visible on the Wayback Machine.[5]

With the vision of a global satellite communication system that could be used anywhere anytime, Iridium's marketing team targeted two main customer segments: international business travelers and     industrial users in mining, maritime, oil, and gas. The latter could benefit from a phone service that was available in remote locations. Compared to other satellite services based on geostationary orbits, Iridium's low Earth orbit shortened the delay of end-to-end communications and used devices that required less power to connect to the satellites.

For international business travelers, the pain point was the lack of cellphone coverage in many areas of the world, and the incompatible standards. They had to carry multiple devices, one for each country they visited. I experienced this firsthand when traveling between Italy and the US — since Europe and the US operated the GSM standard on different radio bands (the US also adopted CDMA, an incompatible standard), I had to carry two different phones. Iridium promised one phone that would operate anywhere around the world.

However, Iridium had overestimated the impact of these problems and underestimated the pace of technological advancement. By the time they launched their service in 1998, terrestrial cellphone networks had improved and were developing in almost every country. GSM was becoming the global standard and new phones ensured interoperability (supporting the different radio bands in use in the US and Europe). Roaming agreements between mobile

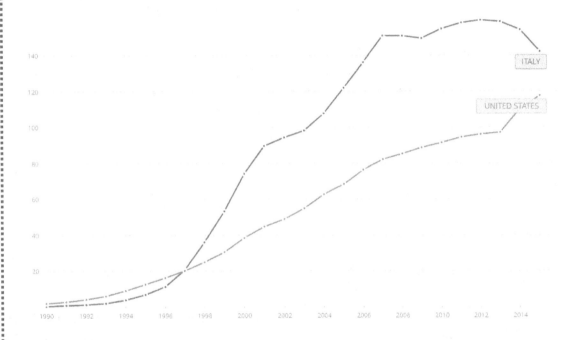

Mobile subscribers 1990-2015, World Bank

operators allowed customers to travel internationally and use their phone in other countries. Finally, mobile cellphone adoption had been faster than expected. In the USA it was about 25% in 1998, in Italy it was already at 36% and projected to reach 100% by year 2001.[6]

It did not help that Iridium had several problems at launch. First, its devices were not ready. It had two major partners develop the Iridium phones: Motorola and Kyocera. Both had developed working prototypes but were not ready for scaling production. When the Iridium service became available, new customers could not get their device fast enough.

In addition, the first devices were bulky, heavy, and had limited battery life. Because they needed direct line of sight with a satellite to communicate, they did not work inside cars or buildings, and often suffered from signal loss in areas with tall structures or large obstacles. This problem is depicted in the scene from the movie "The Lone Survivor" (2013) where the satellite phone doesn't work in the middle of the woods where they are hiding. Murphy must climb to the top of an exposed ridge to make a phone call back to base and gets killed doing it.

The commercialization strategy counted on a distributed network of local partners in every country. For example, Iridium Italia was responsible for overseeing the market development across Europe, and in supporting local mobile operators in those countries. With the support of the mobile operators, this strategy was designed to reach the millions of existing subscribers to national cellphone operators and upsell them to Iridium.

The problem was that these mobile operators were not ready to sell, and support, Iridium. Partners were not properly trained and were not ready to respond to sales inquiries. Customers interested in testing the service found it difficult to get answers or to try a device.

Coupled with the cost of a device, around $3,000, and the cost of the service, which ranged between $3 and $7 per minute, Iridium was an expensive proposition. So, it's no surprise that the Iridium subscriber base did not grow as expected, and Iridium had a hard time raising additional working capital from investors.

Even when it dropped the cost of a device to about $2,000 and offered service discounts of up to 65%, it was not able to gain the broad traction in the market it had planned for.[7] A few months later it filed for bankruptcy.

Over the years, Iridium (now a public company, traded as IRDM) has gone through restructuring and has emerged as a nimbler company focused on niche market segments of industrial workers and military. It has transformed its market approach and simplified its service offering, while creating new services in the satellite industry. In 2017, it started the deployment of its next-generation satellite network, called Iridium NEXT.[8]

This story is based on my personal experience working with Iridium Italia and the sources mentioned in the References.

More information on the Iridium story is widely available on the Internet, and a couple of interesting books "Down to Earth: Satellite Technologies, Industries, and Cultures (New Directions in International Studies)" Jun 4, 2012, by Lisa Parks and James Schwoch, published by Rutgers University Press, and "Eccentric Orbits: The Iridium Story", Jun 7, 2016 by John Bloom, published by Atlantic Monthly Press.

# THE MINIMUM VIABLE PRODUCT OR MVP

Innovative new products or services inevitably push the boundary of what is commonly accepted and enter uncharted territory. This push to take the customers to new ways of solving their problems and doing business is what drives innovation. Most times new products and services are based on a set of hypotheses that are yet to be validated. Instead of releasing the whole product at once after investing time and money, and then realizing that some of the key assumptions were wrong, we should understand what customers value through frequent, short iterations. Paraphrasing one of the principles of the Agile manifesto, our highest priority is to satisfy the customer through early and continuous delivery of valuable product increments.

An MVP (Minimum Viable Product) is the minimum set of functionalities that allows you to validate your product idea and collect feedback. The goal of an MVP is to learn in the fastest/easiest/cheapest way if your idea is valid, and then pivot if necessary.[9] This helps to reduce risks and to keep the cost of change to a minimum. Since the concept was formalized in 2011 in the book The Lean Startup, it has been adopted by organizations worldwide, often as a synonym of Agile development. I have heard phrases like "oh, we are Agile, because we are building an MVP." However, I have found that an MVP is probably one of the most misunderstood concepts and is often used in the wrong context.

Many teams confuse the MVP as building a functional slice of their product, releasing it, and then building the next slice. The plan is set up front, and the product is built one slice at a time. But an MVP is not a slicing approach to building a product. Rather, it should be a learning opportunity to collect feedback and validate a hypothesis as quickly as possible, and then change the plan if needed. The main question an MVP should help you answer is not "can I build this?", but instead "are customers interested in buying it?"

Any work on an MVP should always start with a set of hypotheses that the MVP is intended to validate. Without the learning and validation aspects, an MVP becomes just a small release of a product — or a "Beta release". But when you use it to validate your hypotheses and learn from your customers, the MVP is a powerful tool to explore the validity of your ideas before spending too much time, effort, or money on it. An MVP helps you evaluate key elements of your solution and get one step closer to validate market-solution fit.

If you are building a new car, you may decide that leather seats, drive departure alerts, and sport braking systems are not key features of your MVP and put them aside in your first product. However, if your car is intended for the luxury market, your customers probably expect leather seats. Conversely, if you are targeting the sport segment, a double-disc, four-wheel Brembo sport braking system can be necessary to highlight the performance and driving ability of your vehicle. The features of your MVP depend on the type of product or service that you intend to build, and the customer experience that you want to deliver.

Sometimes an MVP may not be in the form of your final product. Before investing in building the whole system, or an entire manufacturing plant, or a website with a scalable architecture and full redundancy, you may find ways to build a working MVP using available resources and quickly validate if your customers are interested in it. For example, use out-of-the-box tools before developing your custom software; use someone else's manufacturing plant before building your own; leverage a local partner to provide parts of your service until you are ready to do it all on your own.

## FURTHER READING

"The Lean Startup", by Eric Ries, Random House, 2011

MVP on Wikipedia: https://en.wikipedia.org/wiki/ Minimum_viable_product

A REAL STORY

# TESLA ROADSTER

When Tesla built its first Roadster electric car, it didn't build a gigantic manufacturing plant, hire hundreds of mechanics, or establish contracts with a multitude of suppliers. Its first goal was to validate whether it could prove the validity of its technology (new lithium batteries packed in high density) and whether customers would be interested in buying an electric car that represented a choice of lifestyle and status symbol, rather than a utility vehicle (like many that already existed). At that time, charging stations were not as common as they are today, and they represented a big obstacle in delivering a customer experience that was anywhere close to the ease of refilling a gas tank in regular cars. Would customers live with it?

Tesla focused its effort on designing the overall customer experience for its customers and on building just the key components of the new car. It then left the manufacturing and assembly to Lotus Cars in the UK. Lotus was well-known for its sporty attitude, driving stability, and rigid chassis (needed to support the extra weight of the battery pack).[10] This partnership allowed Tesla to go to market in a much shorter timeframe, and with a much lower upfront capital investment, while delivering a customer experience that was aligned with its mission. The Tesla Roadster validated the initial hypotheses and propelled Tesla to become the hottest car manufacturer. Since then, Tesla has invested heavily in building its own manufacturing plants and charging network. It has even propelled into space: a Roadster was recently launched by SpaceX and is now orbiting Mars.

## THE MVP IDEATION BLUEPRINT

So, you have decided to build an MVP. Do you have clarity around your goals? Do you know who your target customers are? What key hypotheses need to be true for your product idea to be viable? What key components do you need to incorporate into your MVP to deliver the experience your customers expect?

The MVP Ideation Blueprint facilitates the process of thinking through all the elements of an MVP. Use this tool to understand the MVP's goal, the target customers, the set of hypotheses you want to validate, and what elements of the Human, Business, and Technology dimensions you need to include. It's always better to define all the elements of your MVP before you set off to building it.

You may decide to test multiple hypotheses and may build different MVPs. In this case, you may want to fill up an MVP Ideation Blueprint for each of your MVP ideas.

You can download the MVP Ideation Blueprint from:

https://www.5dvision.com/docs/mvp/

### Goal/Objective

This is a high-level description of what you want to achieve with this MVP. Having clarity on your goal helps defining all the other elements and focuses your MVP on what you really need.

### Customers

Who are your target customers? It's always better to define a clear segment, rather than trying to "sell" your MVP to everyone. Who can benefit the most from it? Who can be an extreme user of it and help you collect the most validated feedback?

## IDEATION BLUEPRINT
# MVP - MINIMUM VIABLE PRODUCT

### GOAL / OBJECTIVE
What are you trying to validate with this MVP?

### CUSTOMERS
Who are the users who benefit from this product? Who are you going to test it with?

### HYPOTHESIS / ASSUMPTION
What do you believe to be true? What do you need to measure to validate your hypothesis?

### WE ARE RIGHT IF...
What do you expect to discover from your test? What would make this a successful MVP?

### HUMAN ELEMENTS
List elements of the customer experience that you want to test

### BUSINESS ELEMENTS
List elements of the business viability and market-solution fit that you want to test

### TECHNOLOGY ELEMENTS
Describe the form or tools used to build this MVP

Download: https://www.5dvision.com/docs/mvp/

Often, when launching an MVP, you may target early adopters as the product may be too new for mainstream users. You need to define who these users are, develop a better understanding of their needs, and validate whether your MVP delivers on their expectations.

## Hypothesis/Assumption

List here one or more key hypothesis or assumption you have about your product, customers, or business model that you need to validate. The MVP should be designed to collect feedback from your customers and validate these key hypotheses. What needs to be true for your product or service to be successful?

## We are right if...

Next to your hypotheses, jot down what would make this MVP successful. Is there a metric, a specific behavior, or an outcome that you expect to be true? How will you know if your MVP is successful? Having clarity on what you need to measure to validate your MVP helps you avoid making decisions later just for convenience or based on vanity metrics (those that make you look good, but don't really add value).

## Human elements

Your MVP is not just a bundle of features and you should make explicit the key elements of the customer experience you want to validate. These human elements help your product stand out, differentiate from others in the market, and make your customers love it. You may not deliver the full customer experience yet and may need to have clarity on what key elements are essential to the success of your MVP. The trick is to identify the right compromise of the customer experience without a full upfront investment in the final product.

For example, if you are launching an online system that people can use to book rooms in someone else's house, your potential customers may be concerned about the quality of the accommodation and the cleanliness of the room they are going to find. Instead of relying on the host to self-manage its listing (with possibly great variability of quality from listing to listing), you may offer support to your hosts in crafting the listing, maybe making it mandatory to approve it before going live. You may also send a professional photographer to take photos of the house and make its listing stand out. Airbnb used some of these elements when it was still establishing its model.[11]

## Business elements

The goal of an MVP is to learn about the viability of your business idea and whether it has market-solution fit, i.e. not only your solution solves a problem for your customers, but they also are interested in buying it. You need to know what to measure. The Business dimension focuses on identifying key metrics and objectives that you want to validate with your MVP.

To get you started, you may want to answer questions such as: are your customers going to use your product? Are they willing to pay for it? Is the price right for the value provided? Are customers going to refer your product to other customers?

## Technology elements

The technology elements describe the minimum set of capabilities needed for the MVP. What do you really need to make it work? The idea is to build just the capabilities needed to deliver the key components of your customer experience and test your hypotheses.

If customer support is expected to be a key component of your offering (for example, because your product is too innovative and customers may need help to learn how to use it), you may want to define what infrastructure to put in place to provide support. To minimize your upfront investment, you may decide to start with just email support or a single phone line, even if you expect at full scale that you will need thousands of call-center agents.

Tools like Product Journey Maps help develop a deeper understanding of customer needs and identify those capabilities that are essential to validate the key hypotheses of your idea.

# THE GOOZEX MVP

Goozex.com was an online trading platform for video games built on a virtual currency. Together with three other partners, I co-founded the company in 2006, and later sold it in 2012. It grew to become the leading online trading website for video games in North America.

When Jon Dugan went to a local Gamestop store to sell a used video game, he received $35 for it. He had purchased that game new just two weeks before for about $60. He would have to spend the same amount of money to get a new game, in fact losing $25 in the trade. That's how the video game trade-in market worked, and Jon's experience was shared by thousands of passionate video gamers every day. The difference was that Jon decided that day to find a better way to facilitate used video game transactions.

Sure, there were alternatives. You could sell your video game on eBay or Amazon Marketplace (or a variety of other second-hand online markets) and get more money than what Gamestop offered, but these alternatives required effort to setup your listing on the website, decide what was the right price for your product, and then finally ship it to the buyer and deal with possible complaints. And then you had to buy a new game from someone else, without knowing what the right price was and having limited guarantees on quality.

There was clearly an opportunity to invent something new and deliver a customer experience that was easier and left more money in customers' wallets. And the market was potentially big: Gamestop alone generated $1 billion a year in used video game trade-ins.[12]

Jon had the idea of creating an online marketplace where people could trade their used video games for other games. To avoid the limitations of one-to-one matching (finding someone that wanted what I have and had what I wanted), the system allowed one-to-many matching. To make it easier for people to understand the right price of a product and avoid time-consuming negotiations on price, the system set its own prices for all products using a complex algorithm that accounted for demand and supply of each game (among other data-points). To simplify the customer experience and take the focus away from price comparisons with other online marketplaces, the system created its own virtual currency, let people trade their games for points, and spend the points to get other games.

Goozex was born. The name was short for "Goods Exchange", signaling the intention of expanding the marketplace beyond video games after the model was established.

At the time, Jon was a senior at the University of Maryland, and like every other college student he only had little money to invest. He needed help to get his concept started. The two of us met when Jon entered a business plan competition at the Dingman Center for Entrepreneurship, a local incubator at the UMD business school where I was working part-time during my MBA studies. Unfortunately, he lost that competition to other would-be entrepreneurs, but I was intrigued by the potential of his idea. So, after the competition, I reached out and offered to help build Goozex.com. Jon and I immediately clicked, got a little office

Goozex.com's homepage shortly after the launch of the MVP

space within the incubator, and raised a bit of money to get started.

We immediately realized the need to focus our resources and build an MVP. The system was complex, and potentially big. We knew we could not do it all, and we needed to focus. We thought the idea was great, but would customers like it? Would they use our system? We needed to validate the viability of the idea before investing too much into it. At the time, I had a job offer from a consulting firm, and I was still debating whether it made sense to drop it and work at Goozex instead. We needed to validate the idea and do it quickly. We needed to define our MVP.

We knew that our value proposition was built around three key components: peer-to-peer transactions, excellent customer support, and virtual currency with automatic pricing. We wanted to make using the system as easy as possible, to avoid any time spent in creating listing pages, negotiating prices, or dispute transactions gone badly. We needed a database of all video games ever published, so customers just had to search for their games and click a button to offer them for trade. The system would find the first buyer interested in a game and connect them with the seller so the game could be shipped. And we offered a full guarantee on all trades. The cost of each transaction was as simple as possible: a flat $1 fee paid to Goozex. That was it. Compared to Gamestop where each trade cost up to $25, Goozex offered an incredible saving (even adding up the shipping expense of about $3.50/game).[13] But, was this enough to entice customers to use our system?

We kept our MVP as limited and focused as possible. When we launched Goozex.com, it offered just the basic functionality to list a video game for trade, match with an interested buyer, and ship the game to them. The functionality was limited, but the website looked sleek and original. We listed video games for all major consoles, and each game had a rich page with color images and full description. Customer support was offered only via email (Jon and his brother Matt did a great job at making every customer happy). Payments were accepted only with credit cards (we later added PayPal as most customers requested it).

Video games come in a variety of conditions (from new to badly used) and with a variety of accessories (some have just the case with a cover, others have a manual, or an add-on accessory, or even a free gift). Managing all the conditions and options was beyond the goal of our MVP, and we decided to keep things as simple as possible at first: all games would be listed as "game only" with no expectations of packaging, manuals, or accessories. We expected this meant making some users uncomfortable, but it would be a good learning experience for us, and we could always add options and new features later if needed.

We went from business idea to launching our MVP in market in six months. The first system was not close to what we dreamed of doing over time, but it allowed us to validate that the idea of peer-to-peer trading of used video games worked.

We validated the business idea and built momentum within the video game community. After raising some more funds, we later added the option to specify the condition and any accessory for a game, built online customer support features, added additional contents and user-generated ratings for each game, and launched additional services that helped Goozex establish its brand.[14] Goozex grew to become the number one online trading system for video games in North America, and we would not have reached this success if we had not built the company one step at a time, keeping a strong focus on a limited MVP and then building on top of it.

## IDEATION BLUEPRINT
## MVP - MINIMUM VIABLE PRODUCT

| GOAL / OBJECTIVE | CUSTOMERS |
|---|---|
| What are you trying to validate with this MVP? | Who are the users who benefit from this product? Who are you going to test it with? |
| Validate if customers are willing to trade their used games and receive virtual points in exchange. | 18-28 years old, mainly male, who buy new & used video games frequently. Potential customers of Gamestop. |

| HYPOTHESIS / ASSUMPTION | WE ARE RIGHT IF... |
|---|---|
| What do you believe to be true? What do you need to measure to validate your hypothesis? | What do you expect to discover from your test? What would make this a successful MVP? |
| People understand the value of using virtual points. Manuals/Packaging are not important (only the game itself). People are willing to compromise on quality as long as game works. | Customers join :-) Customers who trade once return and trade more. 10% of traders invite their friends. |

| HUMAN ELEMENTS | BUSINESS ELEMENTS | TECHNOLOGY ELEMENTS |
|---|---|---|
| List elements of the customer experience that you want to test | List elements of the business viability and market-solution fit that you want to test | Describe the form or tools used to build this MVP |
| Comfort level with getting points, not cash. Key elements of experience: search, trade, ship, provide feedback. No intermediary control on quality: trust among trading partners supports quality of games. | Perceived value of trading online with points offsets lack of immediate gratification. Returning customers do more than 1 trade per month. | No credit card payment, only Paypal at first. Any dispute between users to be managed via email. Shipping at the post office as regular mail. No option for extras: manuals, packaging, etc. don't count. Only the game itself. |

© 5D VISION · WWW.5DVISION.COM

Example of an MVP Ideation Blueprint created for the MVP of Goozex.com

Since Goozex was a novel concept and invited customers to trade used games using a virtual point system, our MVP focused on validating whether customers felt comfortable in using it and received more value than from traditional brick-and-mortar stores.

Our deployment strategy was a combination of careful chosen steps to grow the market, and to limit the expenses. At the time, we were finishing grad school, and did not have much funding to pour into the company. Partly on purpose, and partly out of necessity, we marketed at first to a limited segment of customers. In hindsight, this strategy helped us validate the business model and grow a very engaged community of early adopters.

**WHO:** We focused our marketing activities on extreme gamers with a high online presence. These were our early adopters and helped us generate buzz on other online communities. We targeted these users by advertising in college communities, at video game conferences, and through press articles in online video game magazines.

**WHAT:** We launched Goozex.com with both the supply and demand sides already in place. We had pre-registered about 200 users before launch, and this helped create buzz on day one. We had also purchased a few hundred video games and had seeded the system with this initial supply of products. When the first customers came, they found a site that was already alive with products for sale and registered users.

**WHERE:** Initially, we kept a geographic focus on the continental US only. This helped us keep shipping costs limited. We focused on one category of products, video games, across the top six platforms of the time. This strategy helped us to control growth and make sure we could offer the best service in a few manageable categories.

Only later we expanded to Canada, and then to Europe. We also added support for thirteen more gaming platforms, and for movies. This allowed us to expand our market by leveraging adjacencies, one step at a time.

**WHEN:** We launched in the Summer of 2006 as soon as our first MVP was completed. We had no reason to delay the launch, as we wanted to validate the business idea as quickly as possible.

**WHY:** Because we targeted cash-stripped 18-25 year old avid gamers, we promoted Goozex as the best way to save money on trading used video games. We priced our transactions at $1, a flat service fee that was easy to understand and much cheaper than traditional retail (where similar transactions could cost up to $25). And we understood that avid gamers also longed to belong to a community, so we presented Goozex as a user-driven community where its users could help shape the service and provide suggestions for its development. It was an appealing message to our early adopters.

# REFERENCES

1.  Geoffrey A. Moore, *Crossing the Chasm: Marketing and Selling High-Tech Products to Mainstream Customers*, HarperCollins, 2006

2.  Source: Thumbtack website https://www.thumbtack.com/blog/building-thumbtack/ pulled April 17, 2017

3.  Source: Wikipedia. https://en.wikipedia.org/wiki/Star_Wars pulled April 17, 2017

4.  Source: Wikipedia. https://en.wikipedia.org/wiki/Iridium_satellite_constellation

5.  Iridium.it on the Wayback Machine: http://web.archive.org/web/20000126171204fw_/http://www.iridium.it:80/en/system/home-m.htm and http://web.archive.org/web/20000226191805fw_/http://www.iridium.it:80/en/company/iridiumitalia.htm

6.  Source: The World Bank. Mobile cellular subscriptions per 100 people. http://data.worldbank.org/indicator/IT.CEL.SETS.P2?end=2015&locations=IT-US&start=1990

7.  Source: Iridium press release June 21, 1999. http://web.archive.org/web/20000122163315fw_/http://www.iridium.it:80/en/news/nuovaStrategia99.htm

8.  Source: Iridium website https://www.iridium.com

9.  Eric Ries, The Lean Startup, Random House, 2011

10. Tesla blog https://www.tesla.com/blog/mythbusters-part-2-tesla-roadster-not-converted-lotus-elise

11. Professional photography was initially offered for free to spark adoption and maintain quality. AirBNB now charges a fee for this service. https://www.airbnb.com/professional_photography

12. This was a figure that we obtained from Gamestop public filings and was frequently cited in articles in the video games industry

13. This figure was calculated as an average of several in-store trades we performed at a few local Gamestop stores with a variety of video games.

14. "Get Games from Goozex", GamesRadar, 2007 - http://www.gamesradar.com/get-games-from-goozex/

# NOTES

## Did you lose a tooth?
## What kind of tooth did you lose?

➤ Add a sticker to the chart for your grade.
➤ Choose a color that matches the kind of tooth you just lost. Here is a guide:

- ● = 1 **Incisor** Tooth
- ● = 1 **Canine** Tooth
- ● = 1 **Molar** Tooth

## Tooth Guide

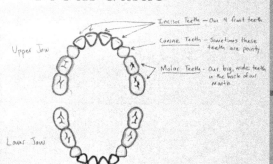

Upper Jaw

Incisor Teeth — Our 4 front teeth.

Canine Teeth — Sometimes these teeth are pointy

Molar Teeth - Our big, wide teeth in the back of our mouth

Lower Jaw

Teeth
Stickers

5<sup>th</sup>

4<sup>th</sup>

3<sup>rd</sup>

2<sup>nd</sup>

1<sup>st</sup>

K

PK4

Measuring the teeth distribution for elementary school kids

PK3

# [11]

## DELIVER

There is no successful product without happy customers. You may get a few initial sales, but ultimately, if your customers are not raving about your product, it will fail the test of time. The goal of product development is to create a product that delivers value to the end users, satisfies their needs, and matches their expectations. A product that customers love.

In this chapter, we'll discuss why it's important to focus on outcomes rather than outputs, and how to incorporate customer feedback to validate the value your product delivers.

## DELIVER OUTCOMES NOT OUTPUTS

The Delivery dimension of a product validates how close you are to achieving success with your product. Your focus should be on delivering outcomes for your customers, not just on deploying a product in the market. After all, customers don't care so much about individual features, they care about the benefits and the value they get from these features. The mindset should be to build a product with features and deliver value to your customers.

## FALLING IN THE DELIVERY GAP

Teams and organizations that focus on launching products rather than delivering value often reflect corporate cultures where the product managers are awarded bonuses or promotions based on the number of products deployed. These companies focus on output. It's the old manufacturing process of getting widgets out of the production line as quickly as possible.

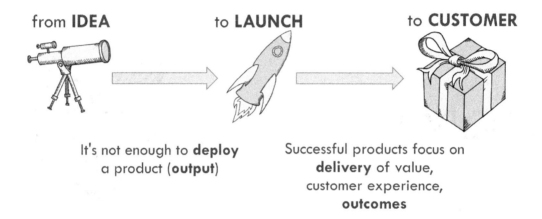

from **IDEA**                to **LAUNCH**                to **CUSTOMER**

It's not enough to **deploy** a product (**output**)

Successful products focus on **delivery** of value, customer experience, **outcomes**

Products should instead be built to deliver outcomes and benefits to the end users. I call this problem the Delivery Gap, the void between deploying a product in the market and delivering value to the end users (and measuring its outcome). This gap manifests itself in several ways, including poorly executed product launches, products that fail to win the marketplace, and products that, once deployed, show a high level of problems that the business then struggles to fix. Companies often struggle to close the gap after the fact.

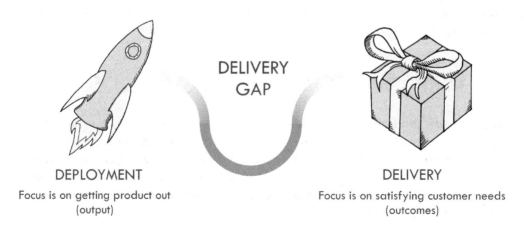

DELIVERY GAP

DEPLOYMENT

Focus is on getting product out (output)

DELIVERY

Focus is on satisfying customer needs (outcomes)

A few years ago, I worked for a company that was recognized as a digital leader in its industry. The company had pushed towards adopting agile and product management best practices and had attracted the best and brightest in the region. The culture was competitive, and product managers were evaluated by the number of products released in the market, causing a rush of deployments in the months before performance reviews. We talked about delivering the benefits that customers expected, but we promoted people based on products deployed. The company had a culture that valued deployment, rather than delivery.

In order to deliver value to the customers and, in return, generate real value for the business, the organization should focus on delivery, not deployment. It should focus on outcomes (for the customers, for the business), not on output. It should create a culture where cranking out products as quickly as possible is replaced with measuring outcomes and real value delivered to the customer. The Delivery dimension of a product focuses on the customers, their needs, and the customer experience (CX) with the product. In essence, it focuses on the value the customers and your business get from your product.

## CLOSING THE DELIVERY GAP

To close the Delivery Gap and create a product that delivers the benefits and value that customers expect, you should focus on the following:

**Understand your customers:** Know who your customers are, what they need, and why they are interested in your product. Too often, I see companies launch new products that seem like great ideas, but they don't know who the target customer is or what need the product is fulfilling for these customers. It all starts with an understanding of your customers' needs, and this drives the other areas below.

**Measure what matters:** With an abundance of data available, you can potentially measure a lot of things. Focus on what really matters for your customers and your business. What you measure should directly correlate to the value your product delivers to your customers, and to your business. If the data doesn't drive outcomes, it's probably not so useful.

**Voice of the customer:** When collecting feedback and data, rely as much as possible on direct input from your customers rather than secondary data from analytics or research reports. Get in front of your customers and talk to them. That's where the real learning comes from.

**Market-solution fit:** You may have a great solution to a problem, but if the customers don't buy it, you are not going to stay in business for long. Validate market-solution fit with an MVP and pivot if necessary until you find it.

# A COMPANY FALLING INTO THE DELIVERY GAP

A few years ago, I worked for a company that sold market research reports online. In the early 2000s, the company had been in the Inc 5000 list as one of the fastest-growing startups in the US. It had done well by leveraging its enormous library of research reports to drive traffic to the website using search engines. People searching for a market research topic often landed on the company's website and could buy the report from there.

Fast-forward ten years and the market had completely changed. Google was the go-to avenue to find anything, from recent news to market statistics. Companies were shifting towards Voice of the Customer activities, collecting feedback and data directly from their customers, and relying on their own primary research. Secondary research, the core of the market reports sold by this company, was no longer the only way to get market intelligence.

Our product was no longer relevant, and we had no idea of what customers really wanted. As traffic dwindled because of shifting market needs, the company's go-to strategy remained the same: offer as many research reports as possible for sale and maximize traffic to the website using SEO (Search Engine Optimization). The assumption was that there were still many potential customers out there and we could attract them to our website by strengthening our presence on the search engines. Sticking to the strategy that had always worked well, we just needed to increase traffic to the website, and revenue would follow. Instead of talking with customers and understanding how we could satisfy their needs, we spent months of hard work re-engineering the website, optimizing our index, and creating a series of original articles to generate new unique content.

Everybody's attention was directed at driving pageviews and unique visitors. In hindsight, these were vanity metrics, because they bluntly ignored the key reasons of our dwindling sales: a shifting customer behavior and reduced value in our service offering. By focusing on vanity metrics that drove no direct value to the business, we undermined our ability to adapt to new customer needs and maintain relevancy in the marketplace. We were focused on output, rather than outcomes. We were affected by the Delivery Gap, and it was widening.

We did achieve some objectives. By redesigning the website and changing the flow of our registration page, we saw a reduction in bounce rate and an increase in the number of registered users. These were also vanity metrics because when we looked at what really mattered, the number of paying customers and the revenue, both were going down. Our service offering was no longer appealing as it once was, and just driving more people to the website didn't result in more conversions. Bounce rate and registered users were two additional metrics that made us feel good but didn't provide any insight on why people weren't buying our products anymore. By sticking to analytics and vanity metrics as our main source of intelligence, we were slowly falling into the depths of the Delivery Gap.

What we really needed was to change the fundamentals of our service to make it more appealing to today's customers. Our gears were not working anymore, and we needed to fix them. From a product development standpoint, we did not know what specific segment of people was still interested in our service, and why (or why not). We should have connected directly with our customers, understood from them what they needed, and changed our service offering in a way that made it more useful to them.

## MEASURE WHAT REALLY MATTERS

With the ability to collect data at incredible rates and access to powerful analytical tools to visualize the data and understand trends, data analytics has become a powerful tool in the hands of managers to keep a pulse on how a product, or a business, is doing. Without data, it's difficult if not impossible to know how you are doing. It's like piloting a plane through a bank of clouds without having a radar: you can only guess where you are heading to.

Establishing metrics to measure and visualize key data on the product's performance is important. The key is to define the right metrics. Too often, metrics are just a measure of output, and do not correlate to the outcomes that your customers expect from your product. What you measure should directly correlate to the value your product delivers to your customers, and your business. You should measure outcomes, not output.

The problem is that we often measure what we call vanity metrics.[1,2] These are metrics that make us feel awesome about the results achieved but drive very little value for customers or for your business.

For example, an online website may measure pageviews, and may even see the pageviews increase month over month. Does this mean the website is doing well? Do customers like it? Is this increase in pageviews driving additional value to either the customers or your business? If you are selling products online and your sales are declining, having more pageviews does not tell the real story. Increasing traffic to the website without a corresponding increase in sales signals that something is wrong (e.g. you are attracting the wrong segment of people, your conversion funnel is not working, or your product is not appealing to your visitors). Ironically, more pageviews also drive server costs higher. Pageviews are just a vanity metric that is not driving any incremental value to your business. Measuring active users (the number of people who perform a specific action) or the cost of acquisition of new customers (the money spent in acquiring visitors before one makes a purchase) seem to be more useful metrics.

The problem with metrics is that they measure customer behavior, but don't necessarily explain why customers are behaving in a certain way. A metric is a number, and in a sense, it measures the symptoms, but not the cause. To answer the "why" question, you need to connect with your customers at a deeper level, for example, by interviewing them or collecting feedback from them directly.

## LISTEN TO THE VOICE OF YOUR CUSTOMERS

Delivering a great customer experience starts with insightful understanding of customer needs and the customer's point of view. Voice of the Customer (VoC) is the process of understanding the customer's expectations and validating the outcomes of your product through customer feedback. Instead of looking at customers through a lens that too often relies only upon analytics, business metrics, and secondary research, listening to the voice of the customer allows the business to interact with customers directly, observe their interactions, and collect feedback. By connecting directly with your customers, you can better understand how your customers view and value your products, discover deeper motivations and expectations for customer behavior, and finally validate if you are delivering on your promise.

I'm not advocating for a dismissal of analytics and secondary research. These tools offer important insights and allow for quantitative analysis of the performance of the product in the marketplace. What these tools often fail to provide is a qualitative look into the needs and motivations of users. They can track and visualize WHAT a user is doing with your product but offer little insight into the WHY. Understanding why users behave a certain way and make certain product decisions is important to design a product or service that satisfies their needs and aspirations.

We have covered some of these activities in the Discover chapter as a basis to understand the user needs. The same techniques can be applied in the Delivery phase to evaluate how your product is doing and how your customers are really using it.

You can listen to the Voice of the Customer through a variety of activities including direct observations and interviews, and indirect feedback such as comments in social networks and ratings of products that customers provide at their own leisure.

Direct feedback

Indirect feedback

| Direct feedback | Indirect feedback |
|---|---|
| Observations | Social networks (Facebook, Twitter) |
| Empathy interviews | Product ratings and reviews (e.g. Amazon's Customer Reviews, Yelp, blogs) |
| Surveys | |
| Focus groups | Product questions to other users (e.g. Amazon's Customer Questions & Answers) |
| Product use testing | Videos (e.g. "unboxing" videos on YouTube) |
| | Comments and complaints collected from customer support |
| | Online forums and discussion boards |
| | Web feedback tools (e.g. UserVoice.com) |

Listening to the Voice of the Customer allows you to shift perspective and view the world through the eyes of your customers. While any of these methods can be a source of validation and new insights, observations and empathy interviews offer a couple of distinctive advantages compared to the other methods: they are in-person, so you get immediate feedback and you can ask follow-up questions to gain deeper understanding.

## MARKET-SOLUTION FIT

Ultimately what you need to validate is whether your product achieves market-solution fit. This is the ultimate test to validate your idea and ensure sustainable success in the market. Here are three questions you should answer to validate market-solution fit:

**1) Are your customers using your product? More so, are they willing to pay for it?**

There is no successful product if customers are not using it. And in order to evaluate if they really care about it, they should be investing in it. An investment can be in the obvious form of cash, and this is what usually applies to products you sell to external customers. But there are other forms of investment from a customer's perspective, including investment of time, of resources, and of other people's attention. If you have built a corporate tool for your internal users, for example, they are investing their time in using it instead of something else.

## 2) Are they coming back for more?

Returning users are essential in business. The acquisition cost of a new customer is usually much higher than the cost of retaining an existing customer. Products that rely on new customer acquisition all the time are doomed to fail, unless the customer value is so high that it more than compensates the acquisition cost. The reality is that most likely you need a good balance of new and returning customers.

## 3) Are they referring your product to other people?

Your customers like your product so much that they are willing to invite their friends and family (or even complete strangers) to try it. When your customers act as ambassadors for your product, they create the opportunity to scale, to lower your acquisition cost, and to generate a network effect where the value to each user increases by having more people using it (think Whatsapp or Waze).

# GOOZEX AND THE QUEST FOR MARKET-SOLUTION FIT

**A REAL STORY**

When we started Goozex in 2006, the process of trading (buying and selling) a used video game for another one was either expensive or cumbersome. A retail store (for example, Gamestop) would offer you little money for a used video game, and sometimes you'd have to add more than $25 out-of-pocket to buy another one. As an alternative, you could sell your game online (for example, on eBay or Amazon) and get more value for it. However, you had to be somehow educated about the market price of that video game, as every title had a different value. On some systems, you'd have to negotiate the price with the buyer, or wait for an auction to close. And when, finally, you were able to buy another game you liked, you'd have to trust the seller that it would ship it in good condition. All these steps represented a pain we strived to solve.

Our vision for Goozex.com was of an online system where users could trade used video games with one another with ease and convenience. A user could trade their video game and earn full value for it in the form of "Goozex points" and then could spend their points to get another title of comparable value. The cost per transaction was only $1 (paid to Goozex) plus shipping, so the out-of-pocket expense was strongly reduced. We removed the need to negotiate a price by using a virtual currency and by fixing a value for each game automatically, using a proprietary algorithm that took into consideration the relative supply and demand for each product (among other things). This also solved the need to research the market value of a title — we gave it to you. We guaranteed each trade, so both parties felt safe to trade on Goozex. We also automated the job of creating, paying for, and printing a shipping label so that a seller could package an item at home and just put it in the nearest mailbox. No more lines at the post office.

This all sounded awesome, and we quickly grew a community of passionate gamers. We went from a few hundred to several thousand in a matter of few months for both the number of registered users and the number of transactions completed. The feedback we received from our users was positive. People loved the service and started to spread the word especially among a few online communities dedicated to finding good deals on video games. On one of these sites, Goozex won the user award for best video game trading website three years in a row. We had started our journey from a pain point and had created a service that proved to be a great solution for many gamers (problem-solution fit).

We soon discovered that customer acquisition wasn't as easy as we thought it would be. New customers were willing to give Goozex a try — after all, it sounded like a great service, and there were rave reviews in online communities — but after trading one or two games, they decided it was not for them. Often, they had to wait a few weeks to get the game they wanted, and even if the overall experience was easier and more rewarding than alternatives, the lack of instant gratification was a pain. The acquisition costs for us kept piling up, as we needed to acquire new customers all the time. With an acquisition cost of about $5 per customer, and a lifetime value of $8, we needed scale to sustain the business financially for the long term.

We tried to build a network effect by giving incentives to people who referred new customers. But even those that liked the service were hesitant to invite their friends. In their opinions, other users meant additional demand for the titles they were interested in, and new users were seen as competitors for the limited supply of games.

The challenge was to reach market-solution fit and create a sustainable business. After acquiring and establishing a strong reputation among our early adopters, we had a hard time crossing the chasm to mainstream users. The early adopters valued the service we offered and the community of gamers that had spun around our service. They were willing to put up with some discomfort, for example staying up till 2am on Tuesday nights to get a good spot in line for the newest titles (Tuesday was the day when new titles were announced). Games in high demand (for example, the latest "Halo" or the latest "NFL Madden") almost immediately built up a long queue of requests, and it took weeks before any of these titles became available on the platform (those that purchased the new game wanted to play with it for some time before trading it used, after all).

The mainstream users didn't want to deal with these problems. They cared about getting a fair price on their used games and getting the next one quickly. They wanted the same instant gratification they could get by walking into a Gamestop store and buy that game today — even if it meant a higher price.

We tried different pivots on the original concept trying to alleviate the main pain points of long lines, rebalancing supply and demand, and finding ways to provide instant gratification. Some of these changes brought a little relief, but in the end, they did little to help us attract (and retain) the mainstream users.

In addition, the market was changing. Physical games (those sold on a DVD or cartridge, for instance) were quickly being replaced by digital downloads. This new form of distribution prevented the buying and selling of used games. Mobile games also started to grow and attract large segments of gamers that before weren't interested in physical games. To these customers, Goozex offered nothing, as our core value was in trading physical games. In essence, Goozex remained a niche service for a community of passionate video gamers.

# PLAN AHEAD

Building a product to find out that it doesn't achieve market-solution fit is a painful exercise. So is waiting to deploy a product in the market and only then planning how to measure outcomes. At a minimum, it will be a waste of time, but there is the bigger risk that by ignoring your customer's desired outcomes, you may build the wrong product.

This should convince you that identifying metrics and measuring outcomes should be an integral part of the product development process. As you go through the Discovery, Design, and Development phases, start laying down the strategy you will use in Delivery to validate the success of your product. What metrics will determine success? How will you collect feedback from customers?

It's useful to think of the five dimensions of product development (Discover, Design, Develop, Deploy and Deliver) not as sequential phases to be attained one after the other, but rather as five dimensions of a product that should be considered together, albeit through different lenses.

A new product should be planned across the five dimensions and then executed in steps. You can always go back and repeat one of the steps if needed, but as you move forward through the different phases, you know what to expect and how to plan. This is the goal of the five dimensions: to provide you a framework that helps you plan a new product through all phases (Discover, Design, Develop, Deploy, and Deliver), understand your needs and the key activities at each step, and plan ahead.

# CONCLUSION

Building a new product or service can be a fun, challenging, and exciting exercise. I hope I have given you enough of a toolset to get you started on your product journey. The 5 Dimensions of Great Products canvas is a useful worksheet to use for ideas and for planning different activities. You have a printed copy in this book (see next page) and can download it at any time from:

https://www.5dvision.com/docs/5d-canvas/

In conclusion, I would like to leave at least three main concepts behind: incorporate your customers and their feedback throughout your product journey; build your product incrementally, learning and adapting at each step; and incorporate in your plan how you will measure the value you deliver to your customers.

Please connect with me on LinkedIn or Twitter and send me your questions and your feedback on this book — the things you liked, those that you'd hoped to see more of, and those that you didn't like. In the spirit of continuous improvement, I need your feedback to validate this product and plan the next iteration.

# THE 5 DIMENSIONS OF GREAT PRODUCTS

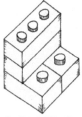

| DISCOVER | DESIGN | DEVELOP |
|---|---|---|
| **GOAL** | | |
| Identify the problem, need or opportunity. Validate concept. | Define the solution | Build the right product |
| **CHALLENGE** | | |
| Fuzzy Front End | Problem-Solution Fit | Minimize Cost & Risk |
| **TOOLS** | | |
| Design Thinking | Design Thinking | Iterative Development |
| Market Analysis | Design Sprint | Scrum/Kanban/XP |
| SWOT | User Personas | Prioritization |
| Blue Ocean | Customer Journey Map | ATDD |
| Value Price Analysis | Product Journey Map | DevOps |
| Conjoint Analysis | Prototype Testing | CI/CD |
| Business Model Canvas | Usability Tests | Usability Tests |
| Empathy Interviews | Empathy Interviews | Empathy Interviews |
| Observations | Observations | Observations |
| Lean Canvas | Scoring model | Product Use Tests |
| Buy-A-Feature | | MVP |
| **ARTIFACTS** | | |
| Vision Statement | Solution Design | Product Increment |
| Opportunity Canvas | Business Plan | Roadmap |
| 5D Worksheet | Prototypes, UI/UX | Backlog |

| DEPLOY | DELIVER |
|---|---|
| Launch in market | Evaluate customer value and collect feedback |
| Full Product Readiness | Market-Solution Fit |
| Market Testing | Metrics and Analytics |
| Simulate Test Market | Customer Feedback |
| Marketing | |
| DevOps | |
| | Usability Tests |
| | Empathy Interviews |
| | Observations |
| Product Use Tests | Product Use Tests |
| MVP | MVP |
| Training Manuals, Sales Guides | Metrics |
| Supply Chain | Market Analysis |
| Customer Support | Customer Feedback |

229

# REFERENCES

1.  Eric Ries, The lean startup, Crown Publishing Group (Penguin Random House), 2011

2.  "What is a Vanity Metric?" - https://www.crazyegg.com/blog/glossary/what-is-a-vanity-metric/

# NOTES

# APPENDIX

## ACKNOWLEDGMENTS

This book would not exist without the support and inspiration of so many people. Good things in life often happen because of great people who go the extra mile to support you and give you the room to excel. I've had many supporters — too many to mention — and I'm grateful to everyone.

Throughout my career, I've had great bosses, and bad ones; great partners, and bad ones; great clients, and bad ones. I'm grateful to every one of them as I've learned something from each and for the opportunities they have given me. In particular, I'm grateful to Flavio Del Greco, Vincenzo Tuttobene, Frank Bordonaro, Jon Dugan, Mark Nebesky, Rudy Lamone, Brant Shuman, Adam Lehman, Dan Goodman, Kevin Rosengren, Jason Tanner, Jason Lamb, and Mark Pushinsky for believing in me. I've learned a lot from you and I appreciate the opportunities you have given me.

I've had several friends and colleagues who have helped out and offered support. To all, a sincere thank you for your generous help. Simon Botto, CEO of DayBreakHotels, and Glenn Shoosmith, CEO of BookingBug, kindly dedicated their time to share their stories: thank you for your inspiring insights and candid accounts. Shelley Solheim at Capital One reviewed all the Capital One stories and kindly offered suggestions to make them suited for publication. A special thanks to Rafael Ormino, an awesome designer and a good friend, who has cleaned up and improved many of the pictures used in this book. And to Arjan Lasschuit, VP of Product at NewNet Communication Technologies, who read a draft of the book end-to-end and provided valuable feedback. Finally, thanks to Mikki Johnston, my editor, who has patiently reviewed all my drafts and provided invaluable suggestions on how to make them better.

I'm grateful to my parents for teaching me to always try new things, and to keep learning. One such adventure was the decision to move to the USA and give a new spark to my career: I would not have done it without your encouragement and support. You are my guiding light and example.

Writing a book is always a gigantic effort, and I'm thankful to my family for the continuous support. I have taken countless hours away from my wife and my kids to write this book. In a sense, we have done it all together. As my father once said, *"It's better to have your family behind your shoulders, than on top of your shoulders."* I would not be the person I am and would not be where I am without the constant support and energy of my wife Deborah. Thank you for being an undeterred believer in all my crazy projects :-) You are the bright star in my life.

# ABOUT THE AUTHOR

A product innovator and digital leader, Valerio Zanini is passionate about creating products that customers love and developing the teams that make them a reality. In this book, Valerio brings together many years of experience in sparking innovation and creativity within teams.

Valerio has been creating products for more than 20 years across a variety of industries and multiple countries. He led product development teams for retail banking at Capital One where he reinvented the customer experience with a combination of new digital and physical products. He did so by employing a strong customer-centered approach across all phases of product development and by developing a strong sense of empowerment in his teams.

Before Capital One, Valerio was the co-founder and CEO of Goozex.com, the acclaimed online marketplace for trading used video games with a virtual currency - before Bitcoin was even invented. He spearheaded the development of the product, launching an MVP in a little more than six months from the initial concept, and continuously iterating the product based on customer feedback. During his early career, Valerio worked at Cisco both in Italy and in the USA, and was instrumental in the design of new products for the telecommunication market. He also co-founded one of the first web development companies in Italy, counting Telecom Italia and Iridium among its customers.

An entrepreneur at heart, he excels at building new products in the early stages of product innovation, where uncertainty and lack of a clear solution are the biggest challenges. He holds an MBA from the University of Maryland, USA and an MS/BS degree in Electronic and Computer Engineering from the University of Rome, Italy. He is a Certified Scrum Professional (CSP), Certified Scrum Master (CSM), Certified Scrum Product Owner (CSPO), and SAFe Certified Program Consultant (SPC). He is also certified IDEO Design Thinking - Insights for Innovation, and Kanban System Design (KMP I). He works with companies worldwide to develop Design Thinking, Agile, and digital innovation practices.

Valerio is also the co-author of *The Spark Engine: Drawing exercises that ignite team creativity*, published by 5D Vision Publishing.

https://www.linkedin.com/in/vzanini/

# NOTES

# NOTES

## GIVE US FEEDBACK!

Please let us know if you love this book or if you have any suggestions for improvement:

https://www.surveymonkey.com/r/RYMVN9F

We hope you enjoyed it!

For more information about this book and to follow our blog, visit :

www.5dvision.com

**We plant one tree for every copy sold**

We are happy to work with ForestPlanet and their network of tree planting partners to implement our tree planting program. Please visit ForestPlanet to learn more about this amazing organization. ForestPlanet.org

ForestPlanet

CPSIA information can be obtained
at www.ICGtesting.com
Printed in the USA
BVHW01*0737241018
530890BV00024B/47/P

9 780998 985411